HowExpert Guide to Music Festivals

101 Tips to Survive, Thrive, and Have the Most Epic Music Festival Experience

HowExpert with Lydia Endel

Copyright HowExpert™
www.HowExpert.com

For more tips related to this topic, visit HowExpert.com/musicfestivals.

Recommended Resources

- HowExpert.com – Quick 'How To' Guides on All Topics from A to Z by Everyday Experts.
- HowExpert.com/free – Free HowExpert Email Newsletter.
- HowExpert.com/books – HowExpert Books
- HowExpert.com/courses – HowExpert Courses
- HowExpert.com/clothing – HowExpert Clothing
- HowExpert.com/membership – HowExpert Membership Site
- HowExpert.com/affiliates – HowExpert Affiliate Program
- HowExpert.com/writers – Write About Your #1 Passion/Knowledge/Expertise & Become a HowExpert Author.
- HowExpert.com/resources – Additional HowExpert Recommended Resources
- YouTube.com/HowExpert – Subscribe to HowExpert YouTube.
- Instagram.com/HowExpert – Follow HowExpert on Instagram.
- Facebook.com/HowExpert – Follow HowExpert on Facebook.

Publisher's Foreword

Dear HowExpert Reader,

HowExpert publishes quick 'how to' guides on all topics from A to Z by everyday experts.

At HowExpert, our mission is to discover, empower, and maximize talents of everyday people to ultimately make a positive impact in the world for all topics from A to Z...one everyday expert at a time!

All of our HowExpert guides are written by everyday people just like you and me who have a passion, knowledge, and expertise for a specific topic.

We take great pride in selecting everyday experts who have a passion, great writing skills, and knowledge about a topic that they love to be able to teach you about the topic you are also passionate about and eager to learn about.

We hope you get a lot of value from our HowExpert guides and it can make a positive impact in your life in some kind of way. All of our readers including you altogether help us continue living our mission of making a positive impact in the world for all spheres of influences from A to Z.

If you enjoyed one of our HowExpert guides, then please take a moment to send us your feedback from wherever you got this book.

Thank you and we wish you all the best in all aspects of life.

Sincerely,

BJ Min
Founder & Publisher of HowExpert
HowExpert.com

PS...If you are also interested in becoming a HowExpert author, then please visit our website at HowExpert.com/writers. Thank you & again, all the best!

COPYRIGHT, LEGAL NOTICE AND DISCLAIMER:

COPYRIGHT © BY HOWEXPERT™ (OWNED BY HOT METHODS). ALL RIGHTS RESERVED WORLDWIDE. NO PART OF THIS PUBLICATION MAY BE REPRODUCED IN ANY FORM OR BY ANY MEANS, INCLUDING SCANNING, PHOTOCOPYING, OR OTHERWISE WITHOUT PRIOR WRITTEN PERMISSION OF THE COPYRIGHT HOLDER.

DISCLAIMER AND TERMS OF USE: PLEASE NOTE THAT MUCH OF THIS PUBLICATION IS BASED ON PERSONAL EXPERIENCE AND ANECDOTAL EVIDENCE. ALTHOUGH THE AUTHOR AND PUBLISHER HAVE MADE EVERY REASONABLE ATTEMPT TO ACHIEVE COMPLETE ACCURACY OF THE CONTENT IN THIS GUIDE, THEY ASSUME NO RESPONSIBILITY FOR ERRORS OR OMISSIONS. ALSO, YOU SHOULD USE THIS INFORMATION AS YOU SEE FIT, AND AT YOUR OWN RISK. YOUR PARTICULAR SITUATION MAY NOT BE EXACTLY SUITED TO THE EXAMPLES ILLUSTRATED HERE; IN FACT, IT'S LIKELY THAT THEY WON'T BE THE SAME, AND YOU SHOULD ADJUST YOUR USE OF THE INFORMATION AND RECOMMENDATIONS ACCORDINGLY.

THE AUTHOR AND PUBLISHER DO NOT WARRANT THE PERFORMANCE, EFFECTIVENESS OR APPLICABILITY OF ANY SITES LISTED OR LINKED TO IN THIS BOOK. ALL LINKS ARE FOR INFORMATION PURPOSES ONLY AND ARE NOT WARRANTED FOR CONTENT, ACCURACY OR ANY OTHER IMPLIED OR EXPLICIT PURPOSE.

ANY TRADEMARKS, SERVICE MARKS, PRODUCT NAMES OR NAMED FEATURES ARE ASSUMED TO BE THE PROPERTY OF THEIR RESPECTIVE OWNERS, AND ARE USED ONLY FOR REFERENCE. THERE IS NO IMPLIED ENDORSEMENT IF WE USE ONE OF THESE TERMS.

NO PART OF THIS BOOK MAY BE REPRODUCED, STORED IN A RETRIEVAL SYSTEM, OR TRANSMITTED BY ANY OTHER MEANS: ELECTRONIC, MECHANICAL, PHOTOCOPYING, RECORDING, OR OTHERWISE, WITHOUT THE PRIOR WRITTEN PERMISSION OF THE AUTHOR.

ANY VIOLATION BY STEALING THIS BOOK OR DOWNLOADING OR SHARING IT ILLEGALLY WILL BE PROSECUTED BY LAWYERS TO THE FULLEST EXTENT. THIS PUBLICATION IS PROTECTED UNDER THE US COPYRIGHT ACT OF 1976 AND ALL OTHER APPLICABLE INTERNATIONAL, FEDERAL, STATE AND LOCAL LAWS AND ALL RIGHTS ARE RESERVED, INCLUDING RESALE RIGHTS: YOU ARE NOT ALLOWED TO GIVE OR SELL THIS GUIDE TO ANYONE ELSE.

THIS PUBLICATION IS DESIGNED TO PROVIDE ACCURATE AND AUTHORITATIVE INFORMATION WITH REGARD TO THE SUBJECT MATTER COVERED. IT IS SOLD WITH THE UNDERSTANDING THAT THE AUTHORS AND PUBLISHERS ARE NOT ENGAGED IN RENDERING LEGAL, FINANCIAL, OR OTHER PROFESSIONAL ADVICE. LAWS AND PRACTICES OFTEN VARY FROM STATE TO STATE AND IF LEGAL OR OTHER EXPERT ASSISTANCE IS REQUIRED, THE SERVICES OF A PROFESSIONAL SHOULD BE SOUGHT. THE AUTHORS AND PUBLISHER SPECIFICALLY DISCLAIM ANY LIABILITY THAT IS INCURRED FROM THE USE OR APPLICATION OF THE CONTENTS OF THIS BOOK.

COPYRIGHT BY HOWEXPERT™ (OWNED BY HOT METHODS)
ALL RIGHTS RESERVED WORLDWIDE.

Table of Contents

Recommended Resources 2

Publisher's Foreword 3

Introduction 11

Part 1: Before the Party 12

    Tip 1: Do as Much Research as Possible to Find the Perfect Festival for you 13

    Tip 2: Watch Livestreams, After Movies, and YouTube 14

    Tip 3: Choose a Large Eclectic Festival if you're Open-Minded and Not Sure What your Favorite Type of Music is Yet 15

    Tip 4: Turn it into a Destination Festival Trip 16

Tip 5: Thoroughly Research Ticket Types 18

Tip 9: Buy Now, Figure it out Later 21

Chapter 1 Summary 22

Chapter 2: Choosing Airfare and Accommodation 23

Tip 18: Take Advantage of Travel Apps 30

Chapter 2 Summary 31

Chapter 3: Packing 33

Tip 26: Pack for Hydration 39

Tip 27: Pack for Emergency Losses 40

Tip 28: Pack to Communicate with your Crew 41

Tip 41: Pack for Making Friends. 57

Chapter 3 Summary......................58

Chapter 4: Preparation of the Mind, Body, Budget, and Game plan..... 60

Tip 52: Set your Lock Screen 67

Chapter 4 Summary......................68

Part 2: At the Party 69

Chapter 5: Make the Most of Every Moment 70

   Tip 58: Get to the Rail for Your Favorite Artist 76

   Tip 59: Your Vibe Attracts your Tribe.. 77

   Tip 60: Let your Freak Flag Fly .78

   Chapter 5 Summary 79

Chapter 6: Act Right 80

   Tip 64: Act with Respect 82

Tip 65: Share 83

Tip 66: Use Your Manners 84

Tip 67: Understand your Impact 84

Chapter 6 Summary 85

Chapter 7: Settling in and Making Friends 87

Tip 76: Set an Emergency Meeting Spot 92

Tip 77: Get Up Early to Get Ready or Go to the Salons 93

Chapter 7 Summary 94

Chapter 8: Keeping yourself and your Friends Safe 96

Tip 81: Keep your Belongings Safe 97

Tip 82: Don't Take Drinks from Strangers 98

Tip 83: Don't Take Drugs from Strangers 99

Tip 84: Remember to Eat 100

Tip 85: Learn to Love the Smoothie Stand 100

Tip 86: Keep Hydrating 101

Tip 87: Sleep Whenever Possible 103

Chapter 8 Summary 103

Part 3: After the Party.................105

Chapter 9: Heal your Body 106

Tip 91: Go Back to the Chiropractor 108

Tip 92: Go Back to Yoga 108

Tip 93: Get a Thai Massage......109

Chapter 9 Summary.................110

Chapter 10: Heal Your Mind.......111

Conclusion....................................119

About the Expert.........................120

Recommended Resources...........121

Introduction

Imagine a perfect world of complete inclusion, acceptance, and love. This world is governed by the principles of freedom of expression, respect, and kindness. There is no judgment, no hatred, and no negativity. Now add thousands of lively, unique, beautiful humans from all over the world and nonstop, amazing music, parties, and fun activities all day and all night long. Everyone is united under the common interests of just dancing, partying, making new friends, and having a good time. Music festivals allow us the incredible opportunity to experience this kind of utopia, even if only for a few days at a time. Festivals have given me some of the best memories of my life and brought me some of my closest friends. My goal with this guidebook is to give something back to the festival community that provided me with the most purely happy moments of life. In this book, I'll be going over 101 tips that I wish I'd been given before my first festival. Most of these lessons I've learned the hard way, but through trial and error, I have finally mastered the art of surviving and thriving in the festival world. The following are my tips on how to prepare for, immerse yourself in, and recover from music festivals like a party professional.

Part 1: Before the Party

Preparing for a music festival takes *a lot* of organizing and planning. From deciding on tickets and accommodation to what to pack and how to prime your body and immune system, I'm going to go over all of the steps that I've come to find absolutely necessary to take before leaving for the music festival. This list may seem a little long and tedious to anyone new to the festival scene, but putting the extra work in before the party starts will result in a far more seamless and care-free festival experience.

Chapter 1: Choosing Your Festival and Ticket Type

Tip 1: Do as Much Research as Possible to Find the Perfect Festival for you

It is beyond imperative to do your research before deciding on a festival because there are so many different types of festivals out there for so many specific music tastes. If you exclusively like house music, you will be downright miserable at a festival that is fully dedicated to drum and bass music. If you solely like trance music, you will not have a good time at a dubstep festival, and so on. The more research you do, the more likely it is that you will find a festival to perfectly fit your idea of good music and a good time. The festival that may appeal to you most may be a lesser-known festival with a minimal following, so don't count any festivals out because you've never heard of it. Not having heard of the festival means that it's not mainstream, which doesn't mean that it's not an incredible festival. No matter how obscure you think your taste in music may be, there is a festival out there somewhere in the world for you. Finding your perfect festival is as easy as typing "deep house music festivals," or whatever you're into, into a search engine and checking out all of the festivals that pop up until you have a solid list that you want to further research.

Tip 2: Watch Livestreams, After Movies, and YouTube

Once you've gathered a list of festivals that fit your taste, a great way to get the feel of the festival is to watch livestreams and after movies of those festivals. In the after movies and livestreams, you can experience virtually what that specific festival was like in the past. You can get a feel for which type of artists will be on the lineup, what kind of people attend, and the event's overall vibe. Livestreams are an excellent way to discover new artists as well. If you're planning to attend a massive event, like EDC Las Vegas, which books hundreds of artists every year, it can be hard to choose to see a new artist over seeing someone you already know you like if they're playing at the same time. Watching livestreams in advance allows you to preview an artist before going to their set. There are some artists that I listen to a lot, but they don't put on an exceptional live performance.

On the other hand, there are some artists that I rarely listen to, but I would never miss seeing live. You'll start to see that some artists, such as Griz and Odesza, are more than just DJs, they're performers, and their shows are nothing short of magical. These types of artists will slowly start to move up on your "must see live" list the more livestreams you watch of them. After movies are not only a sound research method, but they'll get you so excited about the festival as well! I watched the Holy Ship after movies from the previous years more times than I could count while preparing for my first sailing. Watching these kept me so enthusiastic and focused while I spent hours at work and the gym in the weeks coming up to the festival.

YouTube is another excellent resource to turn to for more information on specific festivals. Emma Kapotes has hundreds of very informative videos on music festivals on her channel. Her channel is beneficial for people who are new to the scene and trying to pick their next festival because she makes a recap video of every festival she's been to (and she's been to a lot). You should also check out her very educational "Rave Culture" podcast, also available on her YouTube channel.

Tip 3: Choose a Large Eclectic Festival if you're Open-Minded and Not Sure What your Favorite Type of Music is Yet

If you're fairly (or totally) new at going to music festivals and you want to explore your options, going to a massive festival with lots of different types of music is a perfect choice for you. These festivals can even be fun for people just looking to mix up what kind of music they usually listen to. I have a particular taste in music, but I went to Coachella (a very musically diverse festival) one year and honestly had so much fun. I usually choose festivals centered around Electronic Dance Music, especially house or dubstep, so it was fun to switch things up and see artists like Beyonce and Post Malone that I would never have seen at the festivals I usually choose. Some other extremely popular starter festivals for the open-minded include Bonnaroo, Life is Beautiful, Lollapalooza, Ultra, Glastonbury, and Sziget, to name a few. My best advice in these enormous festivals is to freely explore the stages and stop to party wherever the music sounds good!

Tip 4: Turn it into a Destination Festival Trip

Destination festivals are my favorite. I love to travel. I've made a promise to myself that I would find a way to see at least one new country every three months. I also love music festivals, though, so what to do when you have limited time off, limited funds, and the expensive hobbies of traveling and going to music festivals? Combine them! A few of my favorite destination festivals include Holy Ship and FriendShip, which sail around the Bahamas, Tomorrowland in Belgium, Amsterdam Dance Event in The Netherlands, and The Yacht Week in Greece. A few that I have planned next are Neversea in Romania, Ultra Europe in Croatia, and My Paradise in Fiji. Virtually anywhere in the world you've dreamed of visiting, I can almost guarantee there will be a music festival either there or someplace nearby at some point in the year. If you're going to be traveling far away, try to bundle your festivals so that you can go to more than one while you're there. For example, it takes me two or more days and between one and two thousand dollars to get to Europe from Hawai'i. Tomorrowland, Ultra Europe, and Neversea all happen within a month of each other, so it makes the most sense for me to stay and go to all three while I'm already out there. A few more destination festivals high on my list include Carnival in Brazil, Ultra South Africa, Envision in Costa Rica, and Electric Love in Austria. There is something out there for every music lover/travel enthusiast; all you have to do is fire up that search engine!

I would also highly recommend taking advantage of layovers and cheap tickets between countries close to each other. Last summer, when I was supposed to go to Ultra Europe and Neversea (thanks, Coronavirus), I played with my Skyscanner app for hours until I found the perfect trip: a one-day layover in Paris, five days in Romania, five days in Croatia, three days in Copenhagen, and then another one-day layover in Lisbon before heading home. Paris and Lisbon were just bonus trips that I didn't have to pay anything extra to take. My trips between Romania, Croatia, and Copenhagen were all less than one hundred Euros altogether. The best ways to find these epic layovers are not to search for the "best route" but to search for the "cheapest route." The cheapest route is generally less popular because many people want to get from point A to point B as quickly as possible. Still, if you change your search to find the cheapest, you'll be able to pick from a lot of different cities in which you can have up to a full day layover to explore.

My favorite layover score so far was when I was trying to get from Switzerland to Alaska. My first layover on this trip was overnight in London, during which I met up with one of my friends from Tomorrowland. Alesso just happened to be playing in London that night, so of course, we went to his show, which was incredible as usual. My second layover was a full day in Iceland, which I now consider to be one of the coolest places I've been. I spent the whole day relaxing in The Blue Lagoon and drinking champagne from the swim-up bar. It was heaven. The best part was that I didn't have to spend any extra money on these incredible one-day side trips! So, if you're going to a festival far away, take advantage of this and see more of the world.

Tip 5: Thoroughly Research Ticket Types

Okay, so yay! You've finally decided on which festival you want to attend. Now it's time to look into which type of ticket you'd like to purchase. You'll usually have to choose between general admission and VIP. Every festival is different, so they will have various perks and prices for their tickets. That being said, read thoroughly on the festival's website to decide which ticket type is right for you. These next two tips are just generalizations of my experiences in GA and VIP.

Tip 6: Buy General Admission if...

I almost always suggest just going with the GA ticket, especially if you're low on funds. Even at festivals that I've scored VIP passes to, I generally ended up spending almost all of my time in GA anyway because it's honestly just where the party is at! Even if you do have the money to splurge for that

VIP ticket, keep in mind that at a lot of the larger mainstream festivals, you'll probably just be surrounded by hordes of pretentious Instagram model types trying not to dance so that they won't sweat off their hair and makeup. In my opinion, getting down and dirty in GA is the best and most fun way to go.

Tip 7: Buy VIP if...

Some perks to VIP usually include shorter lines to get into the festival, access to less used and, therefore, cleaner bathrooms, and access to less crowded bars and chill spots. These tickets are usually much more expensive and rarely worth it, especially if you're attending on a budget. The one festival I've been to at which it was incredibly worth it was Lost Lands, a dubstep festival put on by Excision. The ticket was only a little more expensive, but the VIP area was super spacious and on top of a large hill (think amphitheater-style), so we didn't feel excluded from the music or fun in any way. Lost Lands is a pretty intense bass-heavy festival, and sometimes it was nice to get away from all of the mosh pits and madness and chill with our crew in the emptier, chiller VIP section. I think the good vibes in the VIP section at this festival had a lot to do with the fact that the clientele at Lost Lands is not a flashy crowd by any means. Even in VIP, people were stoked and dancing and obviously there because they love dubstep (not because they wanted to have a photoshoot). Another huge perk of going VIP at Lost Lands was their Lunautics beauty tent inside the glamping area. Inside the beauty tent, we could pick out whichever

Lunautics face jewels and glitter we wanted, and a professional would glam us up for free. They also offered free hair braiding with colored extensions. It was such a fantastic resource to have when I was hurting in the mornings and didn't feel like putting in the work to make myself pretty. Again though, read everything about the festival ticket types on the festival website because it totally can be worth the money in some cases.

Tip 8: Do Not Buy From a Stranger Online

Seriously, please don't do it. If the festival you want to go to sells out, I can guarantee you that there are scammers out there taking advantage of that. I have a friend who was scammed out of a little over a thousand dollars last year from people who put up a fake advertisement for concert tickets that never existed. A lot of festivals will have a buy/sell page on Facebook in which you can connect to a real person with an actual profile to buy your tickets. We all know what a fake profile looks like; if they have no friends and their most recent photo is from yesterday, they're trying to scam you. If you have mutual friends, you can see that they have real pictures of themselves from many years ago, and so on, it is exponentially more unlikely that they are trying to scam you. However, whenever possible, buy your ticket early to avoid having to buy from a third party altogether.

Tip 9: Buy Now, Figure it out Later

If you see a festival that you desperately want to go to, you will find a way to make it work! Avoid realizing last minute, after the festival sold out, that you're going to have severe FOMO (fear of missing out) the entire time everyone else is out there having the time of their lives at the festival that you really wanted to go to. I can't tell you the number of times I've gotten in way over my head with overbooking myself for festivals and trips that I couldn't afford, but I've always made it work. Once you have that ticket purchased, your whole world will change. You'll suddenly be picking up more shifts at work, staying later than scheduled, and working as hard as you can to make that money appear. You'll lose interest in wasting money by going out to bars in your hometown, eating out for every meal, going shopping for things you don't need, etc. I had so many festivals and trips planned one year that I picked up a second job and worked eighty hours a week with no days off for months. The crazy part was that I wasn't even bothered by the workload because I was so overly excited about the incredible year I had planned for myself. It is unbelievable what you can make happen when you've made the commitment to yourself and bought the ticket to something that you really wanted to go to. Buy the ticket, manifest your destiny, and make it happen.

Chapter 1 Summary

Music festivals take a lot of work and research. Deciding on which festival you want to go to is fundamentally the most crucial choice you will have to make, so choose wisely. All festivals are not the same, and not all festivals are for everyone. Putting the time into finding the perfect festival for you is one of the most important things you can do to ensure that you have a fantastic experience. Aside from this, you will also have to choose which type of ticket will be most worth your money. Buying as soon as you decide is key because tickets do sell out. In the end, you don't want to be stuck having to decipher whether a third-party seller is scamming you or not if you try to buy your ticket after they've sold out. Most festivals offer a payment plan anyway, so make the commitment and book that ticket! You will only regret the festivals you didn't go to.

Chapter 2: Choosing Airfare and Accommodation

Tip 10: Thoroughly Research all Accommodation Options

For every festival, there will be a lot of options for accommodation. If you're doing it right, you will spend next to no time in your accommodation of choice due to the endless list and tireless schedule of activities and events going on at the festival. That being said, the few hours that you do get to have away from the mayhem, noise, and excitement need to be spent in a place that you feel comfortable in order to reboot. Comfort zones are different for everyone, so I will go over the most popular accommodations, from a sleeping bag on the ground inside of a self-built tent to a quiet and comfortable posh hotel room with air conditioning.

Tip 11: Choose Camping Whenever Possible

If you want to have the full festival experience, I highly recommend camping. One of the biggest reasons to camp is to take out the need to figure out transportation to and from the festival. Getting to and from an event will likely be the most irritating thing you will have to experience at any festival. More importantly, though, I choose camping because some of my best lifelong festival friends were my neighbors at camping festivals. It is by far the most social option. There are usually two options for camping: GA camping and glamping. GA camping is the cheapest and most basic option, so if you're on a shoestring budget and aren't overly concerned with comfort, this will be just fine for you. In my experience, glamping is by far and without a doubt the best and most convenient choice of all the accommodation options. Glamping is much different from your traditional forms of camping. In most cases, with glamping, the weatherproof tent is already set up for you with electrical outlets, a full-size air mattress, and air conditioning. It is the perfect no-hassle and no-worry set up for those looking to meet as many people and make as many friends as possible, which, in my opinion, is the best part of music festivals.

When I went to Tomorrowland, the event organizers planned a full day in Antwerp to wander around the city to bar hop, collect your country flag, do a scavenger hunt and meet all of your fellow festival-goers. I am a huge Guinness fan, so when I saw an Irish pub in Antwerp, I had to stop in for a pint. While we were in the pub, a group of three guys (two Irish and one English) walked in wearing their country flags. I smiled when I saw them because I thought, "How cute," of course, the Irish boys would wander into the only Irish pub in Antwerp! They immediately came over and started chatting with us, and we hit it off right away. We ended up spending the entire rest of the day with their whole crew from Ireland and England. We exchanged numbers and Instagrams and made plans to meet up with them inside the festival. Fully knowing that it would be difficult to find them again given the size of the festival (400,000 attendees) and lack of Wi-Fi and cell service, we said our "see you later"s and hopped on our assigned buses to the camping grounds. We arrived at the camping site to discover that out of thousands and thousands of tents, the guys we met in the Irish pub in Antwerp were in our small six tent circle! It was like winning the lottery. Needless to say, we spent every glorious, magical moment of that festival with our new friends and have since been to both Ireland and England to visit them. The other people in our tent circle were these crazy, fun Swiss guys that brought over a giant speaker that got the party started every morning and drew in a crowd of after-partiers every night from the nearby tents. I could not have even dreamed up a better group of people to have had next to me at that extraordinary festival. It is the kind of experience we would never have gotten had we chosen to stay in a nice hotel. Camping truly is where the party is at.

Tip 12: If You Cannot Camp, Stay in a Hostel

Anyone who tells you not to stay in a hostel has either never actually stayed in one, or they chose the wrong one because hostels are fantastic and so much fun! I've stayed in hostels all over Europe, Southeast Asia, and South America, and ninety-nine percent of my experiences have been fantastic. If camping is unavailable, or if you don't like the idea of sleeping outside, hostels are the next best option if you're super social. Most hostels offer private rooms that you can book for just you and your friends for those that want the social aspect but are wary of loud and sometimes obscene mixed dorming situations.

When I went to Amsterdam Dance Event by myself, I booked a bed in a sixteen-bed mixed dorm room right in the center of the red light district in Amsterdam because I wanted to make friends. While I have no issue traveling alone and going out alone, I love meeting other people when I travel. You would not believe the characters that I met in this sixteen-bed dorm over the week and a half that I spent there. I think one of my favorite nights In Amsterdam was after the last day of ADE when the dorm room was clearing out because the festival was over. I felt kind of sad because I was so alone, a strange feeling after sharing a living space with fifteen other people for a week and a half. I was sitting on the floor, packing my stuff to leave the next day and making plans to bar hop by myself that night. Suddenly, this group of twelve rambunctious German guys walked into the room with a massive tray of probably thirty Heinekens from the bar downstairs. They offered me a beer, and we started chatting. I found out that they were all teammates on a bowling team just there on holiday. I ended up staying out all night gallivanting around Amsterdam with these hilarious, super fun humans, and we had the best time. They even gave me one of their bowling shirts and made me an honorary teammate! This trip was one of the best trips of my life, and I made an enormous amount of new friends, which I mainly attributed to staying in that hostel.

I highly recommend using the Hostelworld app. In this app, all hostels are rated by location, cleanliness, staff, facilities, atmosphere, security, and value for money. Always, always, always research hostels extensively and steer clear of any with too many negative reviews. My best tip for finding an excellent social hostel is to choose the filter that only shows you hostels with bars on site. Most hostels will have a fun happy hour or do free shots at sunset or something like that, and it really brings people together. Even if you don't drink, you will make loads of friends at the hostel bar.

Tip 13: Airbnbs are a Great Option for Larger Groups

If you're going to a festival with a group of about eight or more, then an Airbnb is an excellent option if you all want to stick together and get a great price. While you could definitely all still camp, stay in hostels, etc., it will take a lot more planning and effort to get your whole squad together to enter the festival. Airbnbs are a really fun option because you can all throw in together to get a super nice, entire house to stay in and party at for a fairly reasonable price. Getting a place with a pool to pre-party in every day and a hot tub to relax your aching, tired muscles in every night is a huge plus! If you are renting an Airbnb, I recommend making sure that you and your squad do have the entire house to yourselves so that you don't have to worry as much about noise levels disturbing the other guests. I would also warn you to be very careful about not leaving a mess. It is someone's house, after all, and you could get charged a hefty cleaning fee if the host is stuck frantically cleaning glitter out of the crevices of the home before their next guest arrives.

Tip 14: Stay in a Hotel if You Like Your Own Space

I don't generally recommend staying in a hotel, but it has its benefits for certain types of festival-goers. If you are perfectly happy making new friends inside the festival only, stay in a hotel. If you plan to spend copious amounts of time getting ready for the day, stay in a hotel. If you want to go straight home after the last set of the night to shower and get uninterrupted sleep until the next morning, stay in a hotel. Seriously, there are many good reasons to stay in a hotel, no shame. Hotel people are usually the ones looking good, feeling fine, and laughing at their haggard fellow festival-goers still covered in body paint and glitter, half asleep in the airport's security line when everyone is trying to go back home after the festival.

Tip 15: Book Early

Once you've thoroughly researched and weighed all of your accommodation options' pros and cons and decided which one works best for you, book immediately! Camping usually sells out crazy fast; nice rooms in hostels are extremely limited; that perfect Airbnb with a pool, and a hot tub, is a hot commodity; and hotel prices will only continue to rise. There are no wins in procrastinating with booking your accommodation. Like with the festival ticket, be confident in your choice and make the commitment, book it, and manifest your destiny.

Tip 16: Fly in at Least One Day Early and Out at Least One Day Late

Anyone planning to go to a festival that is far away from where you live, please take my advice here. I fly in and out of every festival I go to from the most isolated landmass on earth, so I know a thing or two about long trips. Unless I'm going to California or Japan, I'm usually facing up to two or three days of travel time to get to an event. There are no short trips for me, and there is nothing worse than showing up to an event jetlagged. That one extra day of rest and getting used to the new time zone will make a monumental impact on how the first half of your festival goes. Just as importantly, it's nice to give yourself one day to recover before heading home. The only thing worse than showing up to a festival jetlagged and tired is jumping on a plane as soon as the festival is over and making that long journey home in rough shape. It is the one night of your festival trip that I will wholeheartedly vouch for a bougie hotel stay. So, if you're going to a festival that's far away, take it from me, and leave yourself some downtime before and after the event.

After a week of raging at sea and living on a yacht during The Yacht Week, I was exhausted, seasick, and couldn't stop walking into walls. I honestly do not think I would have made it through my non-stop three-day journey from Greece to

Hawai'i had I not given myself one amazingly healing night at the beautiful Sofitel in Athens to order room service, sleep, and learn how to walk on dry land again. Seriously, you will never regret taking that extra day to detox and heal before you head home.

Tip 17: If this is a Vacation Festival for You, Plan the Vacation Part First

If you're planning to explore the countries around your festival destination, I would highly recommend doing this before the festival. It is a great time to cure yourself of jetlag and get used to the time change. Like I said in my last tip, you probably won't have the energy to do much after the festival anyways, and you wouldn't want to ruin any part of the vacation portion by lying in bed sick and tired. If you can only take time off after the festival, give yourself a day or two of downtime immediately after the festival. Then you can start scheduling yourself for any crazy intense activities on your vacation like speed boat tours, bungee jumping, strenuous hikes, etc.

Tip 18: Take Advantage of Travel Apps

Skyscanner and Kayak are my two favorite apps for finding good flight deals. If you have a little bit of leeway with your schedule, the plus and minus three-day feature on Kayak will save you hundreds of dollars. Say you want to make sure you're there at least a day early and leaving at least a day after a festival that occurs January 6th through the 10th. You can search for roundtrip flights plus or minus three days from January 2nd through the 14th. It will ensure that no matter what, you will find a flight into your destination at a minimum of one day before the festival and a flight out of the event a minimum of one day after the festival. You can thoroughly research all of the options presented to you and even filter the best, cheapest, quickest, or earliest routes. You'll be amazed at how much money you can save by using this method.

What I love most about Skyscanner is that it gives you the option to explore all of the dates, meaning that you can type in your starting point, where you want to go, and then a color-coded dotted calendar will appear. Month by month, the app will have green dots under the cheapest dates to fly, yellow under the moderately priced dates to fly, and red dots underneath the most expensive dates to fly. Another fantastic app that I use, especially for longer multi-city trips, is Rome 2 Rio. In this app, you type in whichever city you are in and the city that you want to go to, and it will calculate every possible type of transit you can take (plane, train, bus, taxi, rental car, ferry, walk, etc.), how long each of those options will take you and how much they will cost.

Chapter 2 Summary

The type of accommodation you choose will have an enormous impact on the kind of festival experience you have. I highly encourage everyone to try glamping at least once. With glamping, you will meet the most people, have access to the most activities and parties, and won't have to worry about transportation to and from the festival. This option is so superior to me in my experience that I don't even consider any other option when I'm booking my accommodation anymore. It is crucial that you book your accommodation and airfare as early as possible. Rates only will continue to rise while your options will only continue to decrease. If possible, fly in the day before the festival to acclimate and get situated and fly out the day after the festival to give yourself a day of downtime to rest and recover before the journey home.

Chapter 3: Packing

Tip 19: Thoroughly Research Rules and Regulations

It is such a simple but essential tip. Most festivals will have a prominent section on their websites clearly listing the rules and regulations of what will be allowed through security and in what form. For instance, many festivals will allow you to have gum and Chapstick on you as long as the packaging hasn't been broken. So don't be that person who is upset that their thirty-dollar Dior lipstick got confiscated in the security line because it was already opened. It is one example of the hundreds that I could use, so my word to the wise is to plan ahead while packing and educate yourself beforehand. No matter what, remember to always behave respectfully towards the security workers. These people are just doing their jobs to keep everyone safe. They have probably already had to deal with a multitude of overly disorderly party-goers who didn't read the rules and regulations that day.

Tip 20: Do not Bring Valuables

Either mentally prepare to lose, totally break, or at least damage whatever you bring with you to a festival or leave it at home. My educated advice would be not to bring it. I would cry if I sat down and listed out every item that I loved that I brought to a festival but didn't bring home. It is just not the place to wear your family heirlooms or your Gucci sunglasses. Not only do you not want to lose these types of items and feel sad, but you don't want that sadness to bring down the mood of your crew consequently. Leave the things you love at home. I do understand that phones are pretty much a total necessity, especially at large festivals, to be able to keep in contact with your friends. That being said; unfortunately, phones are one of the most frequently lost, broken, or stolen items at a festival, so the least you can do is backup your phone right before you enter the festival just in case. Take it from me; this is not a lesson that you want to learn the hard way.

Tip 21: Research the Weather

Be packed and prepared for every type of weather, but always check on the expected forecast right before you go. Of course, when you're planning your outfits, it's a good idea to look at what the weather was like in the region of the festival at this time last year, but that can change drastically year to year. Anyone who went to EDC Las Vegas 2019 can account for being severely underprepared with warmer clothes for the record-breaking freezing temperatures at the festival that year. Nothing can take away from how fun that year was, but I can clearly remember being close to tears as I started losing feeling in my extremities and could see my breath in the air as we stumbled back to our campsite after the last set every morning. It was also super sad for the people who spent hours putting lots of money into creating their unique outfits but ended up just walking around in a hoodie and sweatpants because it was so cold.

Tip 22: Turn to Social Media for Outfit Inspiration

If you're unsure of what you should pack in terms of outfits for a festival, my immediate response is to tell you to wear whatever you want! Festivals are all about freedom of expression. It is an ideal place to throw together all of your crazy favorite things to wear and feel completely good about doing it. Cheetah print shorts that you love but don't know where to wear them? Going to go great with your favorite bright Aloha print flower shirt! Seriously, anything goes, so have fun! I just doused myself in glitter at my first rave because I love glitter, and it just became my thing. You'll now see me sparkling all over festivals to this day with extra glitter in my sparkly sequin fanny pack to offer anyone and everyone who wants to sparkle too.

I understand that not everyone has a pre-set idea of what kind of crazy, fun festival styles they want to rock, though, in which case I say turn to social media for inspiration. As I've said before, looking at after movies and livestreams is a great way to see what others were wearing the years prior. You can also follow hashtags like #festivalstyle, #festivalfashion, and so on for inspiration in your daily feed. The most important aspect is that you feel comfortable and confident in what you wear. If anything, everything you see on social media will just further enforce the notion that there is no "normal" way to dress, do you and you will radiate and fit right in (not that it's even possible to not fit in at a festival).

__Tip 23: Order Outfits Early__

If you're ordering parts of your festival outfit online, order as early as possible. I often find amusing, unique things that I want for a festival only to discover that it's hand-made in Timbuktu and would take sixteen weeks to get to me. It's also far from out of the realm of possibilities that an item could show up on your doorstep the day before you're about to leave, and it either doesn't fit, or it wasn't what it looked like online and totally doesn't work with the look you were going for. To avoid all of this, the moment I buy my ticket, I brainstorm and start ordering things immediately. Suppose I'm seriously getting down to the wire. In that case, I even make sure that the items are returnable and order certain things that I feel like I absolutely cannot live without in a couple of different sizes or colors and return whatever didn't fit or whichever color I liked the least later. Putting together your outfits a day ahead of time is very important, though, to help keep you from overpacking. I can't stress to you enough how miserable it is to tote around an enormous suitcase full of clothes that you never even wore on your way out of the festival when your energy levels are already totally depleted.

Tip 24: Pack for a Low-Maintenance Appearance

I get it; doing fun, elaborate makeup, hair, glitter, jewels, etc., for festivals looks so gorgeous and is such a beautiful form of freedom of expression. More power to you if you really enjoy taking the time to do this. I want to warn against going overboard, though, and seriously rethink packing loads of hair products, makeup, and so on. I can promise you that if you're spending two to three hours getting ready every morning, you are probably missing out on something way more fun. Truthfully, you're probably going to dance off all of that hair product and contouring powder by the end of the first set anyways.

The one year that I went to Coachella, I probably looked like a wildly underdone fish out of water. Many of the girls I saw were impeccably beautiful, but I didn't see most of them dancing or looking like they were having fun. They all showed up looking like they stepped right off the runway only to take photos and try not to sweat. Don't be those girls (or guys). I wasn't even slightly done up for this festival, but I was completely unbothered by this fact because I was there to party! Let me be clear that I don't think that there is anything wrong with wanting to look amazing and putting a lot of effort into your festival appearance, but when it becomes an encumbrance on your fun, you may need to rethink your priorities.

Tip 25: Pack for Comfort

    I cannot stress this enough. Bring comfortable, broken-in, closed-toe shoes. Picking up a pair of gel insoles (Dr. Scholl's is a great brand) is an excellent idea as well. I will never forget the year I went to EDC in a pair of Vans (fantastic festival footwear, by the way) that I had never worn before. I also managed to forget socks. Keep in mind that on average, I was dancing/walking over 56,000 steps (because I have no chill) every single day and in new, stiff shoes without any socks at all. As you can imagine, my feet were bloodied, blistered, and a total nuisance the entire rest of the festival. Biggest rookie mistake ever.

    I will also never forget my first year of Holy Ship when I decided not to wear any shoes at all because we were partying in or near pools on the cruise ship or at the beach all day. I decided that shoes impeded my freedom to play in the water, so I decided to boycott. By day two, I was in my room picking shards of glass out of my feet with a pair of tweezers. I'm sure you can imagine how inconvenient even slightly injured feet are during a festival in which you're dancing the equivalent of a marathon or more a day.

    Packing for comfort also applies to clothes. I jokingly refer to festivals as fat-camps sometimes because if you're going full force, you're basically working out for up to twenty hours a day. Suppose you can't dance around your house like a crazy person without constantly having wardrobe malfunctions or feeling too restricted in any way by your clothing; ditch it. You will be highly frustrated with yourself if you get to the festival and realize that the sequins on your top give you a weird skin rash, or you have to continually readjust a piece of clothing that doesn't fit you right. Please do yourself a favor and test out your attire before you pack it.

Tip 26: Pack for Hydration

I'm going to bring this up a lot because it is crucial to stay hydrated at music festivals if you want to maximize your party experience and keep yourself alive and well. Dehydration can cause debilitating nausea, fatigue, dizziness, and confusion. In severe cases, it can cause seizures or death. So, please don't take this lightly and hydrate as much and as often as possible. Hydration backpacks are total lifesavers as they can store up to three liters of water. My favorite brands are Camelback and Osprey. You likely won't be able to bring the pack already filled with water into the festival, so plan to find the closest free water station and fill that up before jumping straight into the fun.

Another item that I always pack for music festivals is hydration multipliers. My favorite brand is Liquid IV. These hydration multipliers are electrolyte powder that you mix into a glass of water to drink. Through Cellular Transport Technology, these packets quickly deliver hydration into your bloodstream to hydrate your body exceedingly more efficiently and effectively than water. This little hydration packet is life-changing for people like me who struggle to remember to drink loads of water. I always drink one straight away in the morning and another one right before I sleep at night.

Tip 27: Pack for Emergency Losses

Losses are pretty much inevitable, so prepare yourself. Most items are replaceable, but two things you definitely want to have extra of are your ID and a credit card. Every year, Holy Ship has at least one day planned in which they dock the cruise ship, and all of us crazy people gallivant around an island in the Bahamas and party and play in the water. On my first Holy Ship sailing, I decided it would be super safe to put my ID in my swimsuit top so that it wouldn't get taken or lost in the sand on the beach while I was swimming. Fast forward six hours, and I'm at border control in the Bahamas trying to get back on the cruise ship, but I no longer have an ID, which was later recovered by a lovely tourist (who tracked me down on Facebook) at the bottom of the ocean. Luckily for me, I had an alternate ID in my safe on the cruise ship. I will never forget how terrified I was while I was being interrogated at the border control by some very intimidating Bahaman guards cracking jokes about how they were going to have to keep me there forever while my roommate was grabbing my passport out of the safe. Moral of the story: never swim with your ID on you and always travel with two forms of identification.

Another significant emergency loss to prepare for is money. I generally like to bring several different forms of payment between cash and credit cards. In my experience, having cash on hand will almost always result in me losing that cash between transactions, but it's good to have small amounts on you just in case one of the vendors doesn't take credit cards. I usually like to pack my debit card in my bra (way safer on dry land), a credit card in a hidden pocket of my fanny pack, and at least one other form of payment hidden somewhere in my accommodation. I know I sound excessive, but I really do have a knack for losing important things when I'm having fun. Even if you believe yourself to be far more responsible and controlled than I've proven to be, it's always better to be overly prepared than underly prepared. You do not want to be that friend who only brought one card and lost it on the first day and therefore needs everyone to spot them for the rest of the trip. No one wants to party with that friend.

Tip 28: Pack to Communicate with your Crew

If you're not concerned with getting a few pictures and videos inside the festival, then a burner phone is the smartest thing you can pack to keep up with where all of your friends are inside the festival. I say this because smartphones are the most notoriously lost or stolen items at music festivals. More on this later, but my one-week-old $1000 iPhone was stolen on my first night of Tomorrowland. Imagine trying to fight off the despair that came with that realization that I had just lost a brand new iPhone right at the beginning of the festival. Lose a $20 burner phone? No biggie. Life goes on either way, but you'll be way less upset about the $20 phone vs. the $1000 phone.

If you're like me, though, and you want that one good shot of you and your besties in the festival and that one good video of your favorite DJ playing your favorite song, you will continue to bring your smartphones into the festival for the better or worst. My best advice is to put your phone in your fanny pack and turn your fanny pack around to your front so that you have eyes on that thing at all times. While I don't condone excessive use of phones at a festival in any way, if you are planning to be using it a lot, keep a battery pack on you just in case you get separated from your crew and your phone dies. Another way to keep you and your team from easily losing each other is to bring a totem, especially if you make one that's large and with LED lights that can be seen from a distance. They can be kind of annoying to carry around, but you can have everyone in your group take turns holding them.

Tip 29: Pack for Injury, Accidents, and Pain

If you're going all in, injury, accidents, and pain are imminent. All you can do is prepare ahead of time for this and roll with the punches. Some things you really can't plan for, like the time I broke my finger in a door at Lost Lands and needed a splint mid-festival. But if you're injury-prone like me, you can at least prepare for the most basic injuries. Liquid Bandage (a total must pack for the injury-prone) is a clear liquid that you can swipe over a cut that forms an antibiotic barrier over your wound to keep infections out. Band-Aids and Neosporin are an obvious must-pack for skin-deep injuries as well. Another item that should be on your packing list is Pre-Heels, a spray-on product designed to act as another barrier of skin for your heels to prevent blistering. Even the most worn-in shoes can start to cause you pain when you're on your feet and dancing around all day and night, so it's best to have some Pre-Heels on you so that you're not in pain for the duration of the party.

For pain due to excessive headbanging, dancing, and things of the sort, Icy-Hot has your back (and shoulders, neck, calves, etc.). The Icy-Hot cream works great, but I'm obsessed with the pain patches because I can wear them all day and night, and they will stay on even for a full day of dancing and sweating. DoTerra's Deep Blue Rub is borderline miraculous for sore muscles. I've gone from thinking I needed serious medical attention due to a dubstep-induced neck injury to feeling almost completely normal from just massaging this product into my neck for a couple of minutes. Of course, let's not forget about Ibuprofen, the old-school cure-all for loads of festival pains. If you're consuming alcohol, please be aware and cautious of the amount of any pain-killer you plan to take during the festival.

One last point relating to packing for injuries that doesn't get spoken about enough is that cumulative exposure to the high decibels at which music festivals pump music can lead to tinnitus or noise-induced hearing loss. Tinnitus is entirely preventable, though, just by wearing high-fidelity earplugs. These are not like traditional foam earplugs.

You can still clearly hear the music, but the earplugs reduce the music's decibels, therefore preventing hearing loss. Some of the most popular high fidelity earplugs include Eargasm, Zound, DownBeats, Hearos, and Vibes. These earplugs cost about the equivalent of one or two drinks at the festival, so save your hearing and invest in high-fidelity earplugs!

Tip 30: Pack for Hygiene

Let's be honest; festivals are a breeding ground for bacteria and viruses. Pack as much hand sanitizer as you can get your hands on. Anti-bacterial wipes should definitely be on your list as well; along with the most basic hygiene packing list goes shampoo, conditioner, body wash, toothbrush, and toothpaste. You're not always guaranteed to have access to a decent shower if you're camping, but the least you can do is brush your teeth. One hack for people flying into festivals that can't carry very many liquids is to bring everything in bar form. Lush is a remarkable beauty brand with loads of products that are organic and cruelty-free. Lush is also awesome because they make body soap, shampoo, conditioner, and many other products available in bar form. It is perfect if you want to shave off little bits to travel with instead of trying to cram all of your bottles of liquids into that small airline-approved liquids bag.

Tip 31: Pack for Freshness

Deodorant: wear it! For the sake of everyone that comes into contact with you at the festival, please wear deodorant. I understand that some people may have issues with the unnaturalness of it all. Still, there are a growlingly large amount of brands out there producing non-toxic, aluminum-free deodorants, so there is seriously no excuse for your BO, people. Natural is my favorite brand of natural deodorant because the deodorant works, and they have some seriously spa-inspired heavenly scents.

I met one of the biggest party animals in the festival scene at a Boogie T set on Holy Ship. We were raging so hard at the front together that we accidentally pushed over one of the speakers that were acting as a rail at the set (do I as I say, not as I've done). This guy always had the best vibes and was always partying harder than anyone in the room. When we traded contact info, I found out that he is pretty internet famous for this amazing viral video of him at Lost Lands dancing around with a deodorant stick and offering it to other people at the festival. You may know him now as "The Fresh Raver" and should check out his Instagram @freshraver for more amazing festival content. He's also become quite the philanthropist, using his platform to hold deodorant drives for the homeless. Anyways, my point is that this guy parties harder than almost anyone I've ever met, and he still always smells fresh. Therefore, there is absolutely no excuse for anyone to stink up the vicinity at the festival, no matter how hard you're going. Even if security is particularly rigorous, they'll usually still let you carry an unopened travel-sized deodorant stick with you if you are going to need to reapply throughout the day.

Baby wipes are a crucial must-pack for freshness as well. Not only can you pretty much completely bathe yourself with these little miracle clothes when there is sketchy shower access, but you can also clean off your fanny packs, shoes, and whatever other filthy accessories that have accompanied you through the party. My favorite brand is Burt's Bee's sensitive skin wipes, available at pretty much any supermarket or drugstore. Another product that I absolutely love as an incredible skin refresher is rose oil spray. On top of its delicious aroma and skin-loving hydration qualities, rose oil is also known to reduce anxiety and stress and improve sleep. I love a good Ph balancing spray that I can mist all over after my baby wipe shower. I would also highly recommend bringing a nasal spray, and eye drops to refresh your nostrils and eyes, especially at dustier festivals like EDC.

Tip 32: Pack for Party Hair

This section is of utmost importance for anyone with even slightly long hair. Unless you have it tied back the whole time, your hair is probably going to be fifty shades of wildly tangled by the time you walk out of the festival every morning. I have long, fine hair that gets tangled incredibly easily. I'm talking about the kind of hair that forms full dreads in just one day. I've been so frustrated by my wildly messy hair some morning that I've spent hundreds of dollars at the salons inside the festival to have a professional brush, wash and style my hair in the mornings. So, if your hair is prone to tangles, I first and foremost recommend buying a solid brush designed explicitly for detangling. Since purchasing my Dry Bar detangling brush, I've noticed a significantly less amount of dead, broken hair left over after I brush through it. It's also imperative to pack a softening hair oil and detangling spray if you don't want to lose half a head of hair every time you brush it in the morning. Dry shampoo is equally crucial because you may not have access to a shower with your accommodations at certain festivals. Not all dry shampoos are the same, though. It is one product that I genuinely believe in the saying that you get what you pay for. If you spend a little extra on better products and prepare ahead of time, your luscious lock will still be intact when the party's over. I highly recommend heading to Sephora for all of the best brands in travel-sized hair care needs.

Tip 33: Pack for Extreme and Relentless Sunshine

Most festivals occur when it's warm and sunny outside, so keep that in mind and prepare for this. You do not want to show up on day two red as a fire truck, dodging around into shady areas while all of your more thoughtful and better-prepared friends are out dancing around in the sun. I recommend spraying on an SPF of at least thirty right before heading into the festival. Unfortunately, you probably won't be allowed to bring liquid sunscreen into the venue, but an increasing number of festivals are beginning to offer free spray-on sunscreen stands. Even if the festival doesn't have these stands, though, I can assure you that there will be vendors selling sunscreen inside if you're starting to feel like you need to reapply. My favorite secret weapon is brush-on mineral powder sunscreen because I can't handle the greasiness of most traditional sunscreens. Not only is mineral powder sunscreen way more comfortable to wear, but it will be much more likely allowed in than a liquid sunscreen. I don't see this type of sunscreen sold in stores often, but I've always been able to buy it at Sephora or order it online through Amazon. Hats and parasols are also an excellent option to shade yourself from the blazing sun. In my experience, every single festival I've been to has had a multitude of hats, and some parasols, too, available at the merch stand, so take those relentlessly sunny days as a totally valid excuse to go shopping!

Tip 34: Pack for Unexpected Rain

Most festivals are planned around the sunniest and driest season of the particular region they're being held in because that's the most optimal party weather. The weather does what it wants, though, and often without warning, so always be prepared for the unexpected. Many people pack rain ponchos into their fanny packs or hydration backpacks because they're very lightweight and fold up nice and small. I like to go online and search for fun festival rain jackets with hoods to match my outfits. I'll tie the jacket around my waist and wear it as part of my outfit all day. I can't count the number of times I've thanked myself for wearing the water-proof jacket while everyone around me was soaked and freezing. Another fun idea is to bring a parasol that matches your outfit if you're down to carry it around all day. You can find all kinds of fun ones by typing "rave parasol" into a google search, but nowwearit.com has a great selection of patterns, including neon and blacklight options. Parasols also come in handy during the day if you want to get a little shade no matter where you're standing. Do keep in mind, though, that these can get a little annoying to carry around with you for twelve plus hours, so make sure you're mentally prepared to tote it around for extended periods.

__Tip 35: Pack for Extreme Heat__

Extreme heat will most likely be your biggest threat when it comes to weather. Not only will you be hot because most festivals are held in summer, but you will be extra hot because you will be dancing and moving around the whole time. While there is little you can do to escape the heat, one thing you absolutely must do to combat getting sick due to the heat is to stay hydrated. I've talked about it before, and I'll talk about it again. Stay hydrated. Dehydration is so dangerous and common at festivals, and yet it is so easily preventable. Just don't be that person that misses out on the festival because you rendered yourself so severely dehydrated that you have to be taken to the hospital. This bums you out, and this bums your crew out. Also, don't be that person that dies at a festival due to dehydration. Just don't do it, okay?

Okay, moving on to other things you can do to relieve yourself from the sauna that is summer music festivals. Hand fans are wonderful. With a hand fan, you will not only be your favorite person at the festival, but you will be the favorite person of the people around you as well. It is unbelievable the amount of cooling force those little things have! If you don't like to carry a lot of stuff, some fans are small and compact enough to either fit into or tie to the side of your fanny pack or backpack. There are some incredibly powerful larger fans, though, that if you're bringing to a summer festival, you'll probably never have to worry about finding storage for anyways because you will be using it the whole time. Fans are one item that I love buying at the merch store because they're a relatively inexpensive (usually around twenty dollars or less) souvenir from the festival. If you want to get really into it, as I do, it's fun to order fans online to match all of your outfits for the festival.

Tip 36: Pack for Extreme Cold

The summer that I went to Tomorrowland, I thought I was set; I was so prepared. I had everything from backup onesies and fanny packs to enough glitter for all 400,000 attendees (I'm only slightly exaggerating here). What I chose not to believe was that it could possibly get cold during the summer in Europe. Huge mistake. It got so cold in the early hours of the morning that I would have willingly paid someone hundreds of dollars just for a blanket to walk back to camp with. Again, this ties back into planning for the weather and always having something on you to help you out in any weather emergency. If you're a total pansy when it comes to cold weather like I am, always have something on you for those moments outside of the crowd in the early hours of the morning. A light jacket is an effortless item to fit in a backpack or tie around your waist but will be a more significant life saver than you could imagine when the sun goes down. I would also highly recommend bringing a really warm hoodie and pair of sweatpants to sleep in at night because there are few experiences more excruciating than being exhausted and not being able to fall asleep after a long day because you're shivering inside of your tent. If you're not flying in, and have space, bringing a big, warm, comfy blanket to sleep with at night will be a total sleep game changer.

Tip 37: Pack for your Immune System

Disclaimer: I am not a doctor; I have no medical training; I am just trying to share with you the things that I do to stay healthy and well at festivals. When I got back from my very first big festival, I thought I was going to die. Seriously, I had the flu, strep throat, and a sinus infection all at once. I had to get a doctor's note to take almost two weeks off from work to heal. My second big festival? I took a few more (but not enough) precautions and only had the flu and needed one week off this time, but I'm sure you see the pattern here that I was not taking good enough care of my immune system and was paying dearly for it. Festivals are such a breeding ground for bacteria and viruses that it's almost impossible not to get sick if you're not careful.

One item that I entirely swear by now is the face mask, especially at dusty festivals. All of my festival friends and I were fully prepared when the Coronavirus caused a shortage of face covers. We had already been stockpiling them over the years because we fully understand their importance. I prefer the adjustable ones that hook around my ears because they don't fall down or off as easily while I'm bouncing around all day. My favorite websites to look for masks are iheartraves.com and lunautics.com, but you can just do a search online and find an enormous amount of options to match all of your outfits. My third festival? I wore a mask, and I was fine (just totally exhausted, per usual).

I do like to take a lot of supplements to ensure my immune system health as well. Garlic, turmeric, zinc, and echinacea are my top four most highly effective immune support supplements. I never go to a festival without these four anymore, and they've probably saved me from more painful sick days than I can even imagine. It's wise to pack a day-by-day pill box organizer to make it easier so that you don't have to carry around all of those supplement bottles. Pillboxes are also a great visual reminder to take those supplements every day.

Another huge thing you can do to stop the spread of germs and diseases is to wash your hands thoroughly for at least twenty seconds every time you have the opportunity to do so, especially after you use the restroom. I cannot stress this enough. If 2020 has shown us anything, it's that festivals are a precious privilege (not a right) that can be taken away from us due to the rampant spread of germs. Everyone must do their part, especially in large gatherings like this, to make sure that they are taking the proper precautions to stop the spread of germs so that we can continue to party on.

Tip 38: Pack for Recovery

Mornings can be challenging, especially when you're averaging four hours of sleep a night. Aside from taking my immune support supplements and drinking a hydration packet, I pack several other things to help me recover from yesterday and get me going for the day ahead. I love CBD for many reasons and use it every day. CBD is known to have many health benefits, from relieving pain to reducing anxiety and depression. My favorite CBD oil tincture to bring to festivals is Hawaiian Choice's Active CBD oil because it gives me a nice healing jolt in the morning. The Medterra Good Morning caffeine and CBD oil soft gels are an excellent choice for anyone who relies on caffeine to get by in the mornings.

Suppose you plan on drinking alcohol at the festival and have a hard time with subsequent morning nausea. Some supplements I highly suggest packing for sickness are ginger (in any form, but I bring ginger pills), charcoal pills (just be aware that these powerful pills will counteract any medications you are on), and Pepto Bismol. For headache relief, I recommend bringing Ibuprofen over Advil or anything like that because it causes less damage to your liver, particularly when consumed with alcohol. 5-htp, a natural mood enhancer, is another supplement widely used at festivals. If all else fails, the hair of the dog has rarely failed me in particular moments of inescapable morning-time misery.

Suppose you are going to a festival at Sea, like Holy Ship, FriendShip, or The Yacht Week. In that case, I highly recommend bringing Dramamine or getting a prescription from your doctor for a Scopolamine patch to avoid having to try to recover from seasickness. I had been on three Holy Ship sailings and multiple booze cruises around Hawai'i before I attended The Yacht Week and never had an issue with seasickness. What I didn't think about is that there is a massive difference between being on a giant cruise ship for seven days or being on a small booze cruise for a couple of hours and living on a yacht for seven days. I woke up so violently ill from Greece's rough waters almost every morning of Yacht Week that I couldn't even get out of bed until we got to the island party. I know some people who even get seasick on the giant cruise ships but didn't realize it until it was too late. The moral of the story is never to assume that you don't get seasick because you've been on boats before. Be prepared with Dramamine at least, just in case, so there is no need for next morning's recovery. Take it from me; recovering from seasickness is immeasurably more difficult than recovering from a hangover. If you already know that you get seasick, ask your doctor about Scopolamine. It's a tiny patch that you stick behind your ear that prevents motion sickness for three days per patch, and I absolutely swear by it now.

Tip 39: Pack for Sleep

Anyone who knows me is laughing right now because my motto has always been that I will sleep when I'm dead (I even put this on one of my Ship wristbands one year). Contrarily though, I do recognize the importance of getting at least a few hours of sleep a night. Sleeping can be particularly hard at festivals because there is something fun happening 24/7 if you're camping, but you just have to pick and choose what is most valuable to you. Do you want to stay up until 8 am, just talking story with your neighbors, only to accidentally sleep through Claude Vonstroke's set at the beach at noon? No! You'll be devastated. Do you want to miss a couple of activities to get a nap in during the day so you can make Fisher's sunrise sermon from 4 am-9 am? Yes, yes, you do because, at some point, your body is going to send you to bed no matter what you do to combat it. It's all about prioritizing and time management with your sleep schedule.

If you're camping, you're going to want to pack a sleep mask and noise-canceling earplugs at the bare minimum. Camps are always bright and loud, and you'll need to put some extra work into falling asleep in that environment. Melatonin is another highly effective supplement to have to help regulate your new irregular sleep schedule. Just be careful not to overdo the melatonin because it can leave you feeling groggy when you wake up if you take too much. Again, I swear by CBD oil for most ailments. The Calm tincture from Hawaiian Choice CBD is one of the most highly effective remedies that I've ever used for my Insomnia. I highly recommend this tincture to calm a racing mind that's refusing to go to sleep when you want it to. If noise tremendously irritates you when you're trying to sleep, I'm 100% with you. When the music is pounding in the campgrounds, but I know I need to sleep for a bit, I just put in my noise-canceling headphones and turn up my White Noise app to the point at which I can't hear anything but the white noise, and I can sleep through pretty much anything. At the end of the day, no matter how invincible you (think you) may be, you will have to sleep at some point if you want to make it to all of the most important events.

Tip 40: Pack for Fast, Cheap Energy

Festival food can be pretty costly, so if you're ballin' on a budget or even if you just don't want to take the time to sit down and eat three times during the festival, you can pack your food for breakfast in your accommodation. This way, you can eat one cheap, nutritious meal before you head into the festival. It's vital to consume enough protein and carbohydrates to keep you going during these extremely long hours of bouncing around from set to set. Nuts and granola bars are a great and compact way to get a lot of energy into your body quickly. Peanut butter snacks and protein bars are always a good idea to replenish your muscles at a festival when you're up and essentially working out twelve to twenty hours a day. One fruit and nut bar brand that I love is the KIND brand. KIND is a company that you can feel good about buying from because they use whole food ingredients and no artificial flavors or preservatives.

Festival food is honestly really delicious, but it can be challenging to find a healthy meal in there. It is in part why it's so important to eat a big and nutrient-dense breakfast before you start partying and have to essentially choose between a burger and nachos for your other meals. However you decide to eat, just remember that carbs and protein are your friends in this environment.

Tip 41: Pack for Making Friends

One of the many traditions that make Shipfam (people that have been to Holy Ship or FriendShip) so unique and extraordinary is that we always bring little gifts to pass out to each other on Ship. People make custom stickers, t-shirts, bottle openers, keychains, the list goes on. Probably the most common thing given out every year is wristbands. My boyfriend and I make a new one every year with our info and some sort of Ship pun on them. For instance, last year's FriendShip wristband said: "Ooh This Ship Be Hittin Different" (in reference to the Griz and Subtronics song) on one side, "Hawai'i Friends" on the other side, and then our Instagram handles on the inside so that the people we met could stay in touch with us after the festival. It is such a fun and surprisingly inexpensive way to keep in touch with everyone you meet at the festival.

Another thing that a lot of people do at festivals is to bring their totems. Some of our favorite festival friends that we try to always meet up with have this unique totem of Will Farrell's face as Buddy the Elf mid-scream with these hilarious LED light eyes. Whenever we're hanging out with them at a festival, they constantly have people coming up to them to comment on their totem (pretty sure that's how we met them too). Now, whenever we're at the same festival, it's easy to find them because we can spot that totem from a mile away.

One year at the airport in Hawai'i, I bought a gigantic stuffed pineapple to bring into the festival on my way to EDC. Strange impulse purchase, I know, but it just seemed like a good idea at the time. Anyways, Gary, the party pineapple, never left my side during all of EDC, and people's reactions to him were hysterical. Everyone wanted to meet him and hug him and dance around with him. By day four, people we didn't even remember meeting would start excitedly screaming "Gary!" at us when we walked by. Entirely ridiculous, yes, but we inadvertently made a lot of friends during that festival through Gary, the giant stuffed party pineapple. Even if you don't want to spend the money on hundreds of wristbands or a fifty-dollar stuffed animal, there are plenty of other things you can pack to make friends. Items like a speaker that you can blast music out of to get the party going in the mornings or extra glitter to bedazzle stranger's faces with.

Chapter 3 Summary

I know it's a lot, but I've either direly needed every single item on this list or just been eternally grateful that I've had it at some point in all of my time at festivals. The following is a condensed list of the items I consider non-negotiable if you're planning to pack extremely lightly. First and foremost, you must have comfortable, broken-in, closed-toed shoes. At the bare minimum, you will need your toothbrush and toothpaste, soap, baby wipes, deodorant, and sunscreen for toiletries. You will need your ID, money (cash and cards), and backups of both. To stay healthy, you will need a face mask, hand sanitizer, and immune system support supplements; to stay hydrated, you will need a hydration backpack and hydration multiplying packets. For pain and injury, you will need ibuprofen, Icy Hot, Band-Aids, and a liquid bandage.

Chapter 4: Preparation of the Mind, Body, Budget, and Game plan

Tip 42: Save Exponentially More than you Think you'll Need

Festivals are expensive. Between food, drinks, and merchandise, you can easily accidentally spend way more than you had ever thought possible in a day. Yes, there are ways to make the festival relatively inexpensive for yourself, but you will have a better experience if you've saved enough to feel like money isn't something to be concerned about. I travel and go to so many festivals that I've made it just a part of my life to live as frugally as possible and work as much as possible while I'm home. I live like this mainly because I like to live as frivolously and as carefree as possible when I'm on vacation. For instance, I rarely spend more than twenty dollars on a bottle of wine when I'm at home, but when I'm on vacation, I don't even think twice about spending twenty plus dollars on a single glass of wine at the airport bar. Food, drinks, and merchandise are all grandiosely more expensive inside the festival than in real life, but it feels so freeing to have so much saved that your finances do not hold you back. Future-you will thank frugal-you for allowing festival-you to be able to wake up and get whatever overly priced smoothie you're craving that morning and to be able to get whatever souvenirs you want at the merch store and so on.

Daily cash flow needs vary significantly from human to human and also from festival to festival. I like to always have enough in my account to support my spending needs of up to three hundred dollars per day because I'm a little superfluous like that. Still, truthfully it is entirely possible, and not even difficult for some people, to only spend fifty to a hundred dollars a day. I just always err on the side of caution so that I'm not stuck asking my friends to borrow money towards the end of the festival.

Tip 43: Work on your Cardio

It is one of my most essential tips in this book. I've been to festivals very in shape, and I've been to festivals very out of shape, and it makes a vast difference in how much fun my body allows me to have. When I don't do enough cardio before a festival, there are noticeable limitations on how much my body can do and how much more rest I need. Equally as bad, after day one, I pretty much stay sore for the entire rest of the festival because I'm continually trying to go harder than what I had prepared my body for previously. I walk six to eight miles a day just for my job, and trust me, walking a lot is not even close to enough physical preparation. If you're able to get out and hike, I think that's the best way to get a lot of cardio in with incline included. Hiking is awesome because you don't notice you're exercising when you're out somewhere beautiful. For everyone that doesn't have access to hikes, stairs at the gym are my second favorite way to get in shape for a festival because it's not only great cardio, but stairs also build your quads, glutes, and calves (all of which are essential dancing muscles). If you're more of a treadmill person, alternating between running and walking on a high incline will help prepare your body as well. If you don't have access to hikes or the gym, home workout videos through YouTube or various other workout apps are great options. Whatever you do, just make sure you're getting a lot of good cardio and incline workouts done starting at least a month before the festival.

Tip 44: See a Chiropractor Beforehand

It may be a controversial tip, but again this is just what works for me. For anyone who has never seen a chiropractor, I recommend that you do your research first to come to your own conclusion about the safety and efficacy of seeing one. A chiropractor is essentially trained to relieve pain or discomfort in muscles and joints through spinal manipulations. It is something that I've found incredibly beneficial before and after extremely long plane rides and festivals. I get adjusted once a month. I always try to plan my appointments to have one a few days prior (as opposed to right before, due to occasional soreness after adjustments) and one right after a music festival.

Tip 45: Do Yoga

Yoga is a highly beneficial practice for a variety of different reasons. Many festivals that I've been to have free yoga classes that you can attend every morning in the campgrounds. EDC even offered goat yoga the last time I went! A few of the many qualities of yoga that will assist you in preparing for the festival are that it builds muscle strength, promotes flexibility to prevent injuries, and boosts your immune system. Yoga can be kind of expensive, but it's not something that I would encourage trying to teach yourself to do. Many yoga studios will offer a week of free yoga to try out their classes. If you lack the funds, take advantage of that free week to have a live instructor to help you with your form and breathing techniques. After that free week, you'll at least have the basic knowledge of how to do things correctly, and then you can practice yoga in your own home by yourself. There is a multitude of instructional YouTube videos that you can watch for free as well. If you get really into it, there are a lot of different yoga apps that you can download that are still very inexpensive. Asana Rebel is probably my favorite app because it includes several different levels of yoga and offers several different levels of other home workouts.

Tip 46: Get a Massage

Okay, I know I'm starting to sound a little bougie and excessive with it at this point, but massages are not only an excellent, relaxing way to start your wild festival trip, but they do offer actual health benefits as well. Massages improve blood circulation, which is particularly important after you've been cramped up on a long plane or car ride to the festival. Massages also stimulate the lymphs, which enhances immunity and eliminates toxins. I love massages before festivals because they reduce anxiety and depression and promote better sleep to get you into a nice clear headspace. After a massage, I always walk out on clouds feeling like the calmest and most level-headed version of myself, which is a great way to waltz into the party. It is recommended that you drink a lot of water after a massage in order to move the toxins released during your massage out of your body.

Tip 47: Prepare Your Immune System

First, get as much sleep as you can before the festival because you will not want to sleep much while you're there. Sleeping is like charging your personal party battery. If you show up on a fifty percent charge, your party battery will start to die after a few days at the festival. Eventually, you are going to crash involuntarily. One of the most significant benefits of showing up to a festival feeling one hundred percent is that you will have a more highly functioning immune system, which is incredibly essential. Another way to prepare your immune system so that it operates at full force is to nourish your body with healthy foods and supplements. Eat as many fruits and vegetables as you can get your hands on before you leave. Consuming a lot of extra antioxidants and vitamins in the weeks before you start partying will give you a significant advantage in warding off festival-induced illnesses.

Tip 48: Print and Laminate the Lineup

I know this sounds super old-school, but I actually prefer this method over having to pull up the lineup on my phone every thirty minutes. It is also a perfect option for anyone who chooses to leave their phone in their accommodation altogether. Lamination is vital, though, to keep that schedule intact. You can get something laminated in a lot of places, including FedEx, UPS, or office supply stores such as Staples. Side note, if you are going to go phoneless and use the laminated lineup method, make sure that you're wearing a watch. That schedule means absolutely nothing to you if you have no idea what time it is.

Tip 49: Make a Schedule with your Crew

The most exciting moment before actually leaving for the festival is the set schedule drop. This drop usually happens about a month before the festival, so you have plenty of time to get together with your crew and decide which artists you have to see and which artists you're going to choose when they have conflicting set times with another artist you love. I usually stray from this plan at least slightly every single day, but it's always good to attempt to do at least a little bit of planning. There have been many times in which I'm walking to see an artist that I already know that I love, but the music sounds really good at a stage on the way there, so I stop there and discover a new artist that I had initially not planned to see. Never be afraid to stray from your schedule; it's just there for suggestive guidance, but mainly, it's just fun to get together with your crew and have a planning party.

Tip 50: Download the Festival App

Most festivals will have an app available for free for your smartphone. In their simplest form, these apps include the most updated information, such as a change in set times, emergency notifications, interactive maps, and the festival lineup. One feature to be sure to take advantage of, if it's offered, is the interactive lineup feature in which you select which artists you want to see most, and a buzzer will go off on your phone, alerting you that that artist is about to play so that you never miss a thing. A few other cool features that I've seen on festival apps include real-time lost and found, the option to add credit to your wristband for cashless payment festivals, and a list of bars and restaurants with directions from where you are.

Tip 51: Devise a Buddy System

Festivals are very chaotic, but in the best way ever. It's like a madhouse of love, happiness, and beautiful humans. That being said, if you get separated from the group, you honestly may not find them again until you all make it back to your accommodation in the morning. Imagine my panic when I stepped out of the restroom into a festival of hundreds of thousands of people in a foreign country, and I could not find my friends. Imagine my horror when I opened my fanny pack to call them only to find that my phone had been stolen out of my fanny pack. It was scary for me for a moment until I made peace with it, then moved along and partied on my own. It was much more frightening for my poor friends, who constantly had in the back of their minds that something worse may have happened to me, but they couldn't do anything about it. Don't do this to yourself, but more importantly, don't do this to your friends. Especially in huge festivals like this, it is so crucially important not to wander off and not willingly let someone wander off, even if they're just going to the restroom thirty feet away. You just never know if your easily distracted friend is going to manage to get themselves lost in their thirty-foot journey to the bathroom and back.

Tip 52: Set your Lock Screen

If you're one to leave your things scattered around the festival grounds absentmindedly, this tip is for you. Yes, I did get my phone stolen at Tomorrowland, but most festival people are outstanding people who believe firmly in treating others the way they would like to be treated. If one of these lovely people finds your phone on the ground, I can guarantee that they will turn it into the lost and found. If you want to save said sweet person and yourself a trip to the lost and found, set your lock screen as the name phone number of at least one other (responsible) person in your crew. Even if they don't want to take the time to find you, they can at least ease your mind and text your friend that your phone has been recovered and that they'll take it to the lost and found when they can.

__Chapter 4 Summary__

It is so important to get your mind, body, budget, and game plan on point before you leave for the festival. To prepare your mind and body, get as much rest as possible, eat loads of fruits and veggies, take your immune support supplements, and do cardio workouts every single day. To prepare your budget, do your best to work and save as much as possible, especially the couple of months leading up to the festival. Always bring more money than you can fathom needing to avoid borrowing from other people because festivals are expensive. Lastly, get your crew together to plan out a schedule and devise the type of buddy system you would like to implement in the festival.

Part 2: At the Party

You are finally at the party, and it's go time! You are prepared and ready to party, but you have to understand that some underlying party rules are necessary to adhere to in order to ensure an amazing experience for yourself and everyone around you. From staying positive and open-minded to treating everyone with love and respect to keeping yourself and your friends safe, there is an unspoken code of conduct that all festival-goers must do their part in following to keep the festival world as pure and idealistic as we can. In this part, I'm going to go over these guidelines and everything else that you can do once you're at the party to have the most optimal and fun festival experience possible.

Chapter 5: Make the Most of Every Moment

Tip 53: Leave any Negative Energy at Home

Woo! You made it to the festival! After months of planning and organizing, you have finally arrived at the happiest place on earth. At this point, it is 100% essential to decide to leave every negative thought and feeling back with your home life because Debbie Downer is super not invited to the festival. This is festival life, and there is no time for negativity. Having a positive mindset is a choice that you have to make and stick to. It's all about manifesting your destiny and deciding that you will have the best weekend/week of your life no matter what happens. This kind of untouchable and relentless positivity spreads like wildfire, and you'll notice everyone around you will be feeling it too. Remaining optimistic is absolutely imperative for a fantastic festival experience not just for you but for everyone you come into contact with as well.

Tip 54: Go with the Flow

I hate to break this to you, but even if you follow my dauntingly extensive list of preparations in part one, things will still go wrong. Once you accept this fact and decide to adopt an attitude of positivity, very little can affect you. Your outfit fell apart? There are tons of merch stands at the festival selling beautiful clothing. Your favorite artist's set got canceled? Great time to explore and find new artists you've never heard of. Your phone got stolen? Being entirely disconnected from the outside world can be the most freeing way to experience a festival anyways. Did you break your finger in the bathroom door? At least it wasn't your whole hand! There is almost always a way to turn around a situation that you perceive as being negative and either fix it or make the most of it and realize that things could be worse. The happiest people aren't just happy because nothing has gone wrong for them. The happiest people are happy because they decided not to cry over spilled milk and moved along with the fun-having no matter what.

When the mainstage got shut down at EDC due to extreme wind conditions right before Get Real and RL Grime (two of the artists we were the most excited to see that year) were about to go on, we were admittedly bummed out for half of a second. Half of a second later, we decided just to say, "whatever, no time to be sad, let's go ride some carnival rides." The ride that we wanted to go on to ended up being right by the stage that Noizu (who we'd never seen before at that point) was playing at, and it ended up being one of our favorite sets of the whole festival. Riding rides while we listened to Noizu became one of our favorite memories of that festival, and Noizu became one of our new favorite artists. Everything will always turn out to be fun if you decide to just go with the flow and make the best of every situation.

Tip 55: Just Say Yes

The festival world is an ideal setting to try new things, discover new music, make new memories, and do something that you would usually not say yes to. Having the attitude of being up for and open to everything will enhance your festival experience immeasurably. Saying yes allows you to step outside of the confines of who you restrict yourself to be in everyday life. You could discover a whole side to yourself in this kind of setting by just embracing the moment and participating in all of the amazing things going on around you. Some of my favorite festival memories are times when I've said yes to something crazy and ended up having the most legendary time because of it.

One of the strangest but best nights/days of my life was during the Amsterdam Dance Event at a club called "De School." One of my good friends that I met while he was DJing at one of my hostels in the Philippines happened to be from the Netherlands and is well-connected and very involved in the nightlife scene there. After a mind-blowingly fun night at the festival, my friend asked me if I was up for going somewhere kind of crazy. Obviously, I had vowed to say yes to everything during ADE. When in Amsterdam, right? So, we get into the cab and pull up to an old schoolhouse with a mile-long line of people waiting outside in the cold to get it in. Luckily for us, my friend knew everyone there, so we walked right past the line and into an experience so wildly unique, it's difficult for me to even articulate, but I'll try.

First off, let me tell you that "De School" is open seven days a week, twenty-four hours a day. There are no windows, no clocks, and no phones allowed. I truly have no idea how long we were in there for; I just know it was daylight at least a day or two later when we stumbled out into the unforgiving sunlight. Every room was playing a different type of techno music, and every room held something equally as confusing and extraordinary as the last. My favorite space was at the bottom level. This level was extraordinarily smoky and almost completely pitch black, with only the small illuminating flashes of green lasers. The DJ played this incredible hard-core garage techno at such a loud decibel that you could consider the space as sensory deprivation, considering we couldn't see anything either. Scattered around this room were these large black boxes that three or four people could fit in to chill out from the madness for a little bit. We could see smoky shadows of people outside of the box, but other people couldn't see in. We sat in that box and laughed at strangers for hours as we watched their wacky shadows dancing wildly in the smoke and laser-filled dungeonesque room.

In another room, there was just this big green light projected in the middle. We sat on the ground in this room, for I don't even know how many hours watching what all of the party-goers would do with the green light, and it was hilarious. Some people came in and tried to dance with it and then abruptly left when it didn't dance back. Some people came in by themselves and just sat down and stared at it for extended periods. Everyone did something continuously weirder; it felt like we were watching an extravagant social experiment.

In another strange room, there was an arch and a line of people. An eerie voice came over the loudspeaker and asked, "Do you?" and two people in line would hold hands, jump through the arch and shout, "I do," and then everyone would just break into explosive applause for them.

The smoking room seemed almost normal(ish) until a group of what appeared to be six intricately dressed priests came in and started singing in unison in Dutch. They began walking through the crowd offering random people a drink from a goblet containing some mysterious liquid. They were gone as quickly as they came in, and no one seemed to bat an eyelash over the incident. I could go on forever about all of the insanely surreal things that I experienced in there, but I will spare you. Anyways, I completely lost myself in this bizarre space and fully participated in every single zany thing going on without a second thought, and it was one of my favorite nights/days of my life. So, just say yes! You never know what kind of wild places it might take you.

Tip 56: Be Open to New Music and New Artists

My boyfriend and I love Chris Lake. We've seen so many Chris Lake sets that I've entirely lost count. We pretty much wouldn't miss him to see any other artist in the world. One year on Holy Ship, we were sprinting to his set from the other side of the boat when we ran past Saymyname, who we'd never heard before. Saymyname's set was sounding so good that we ended up just stopping immediately and made the decision to stay at that stage for his set. That Saymyname set was one of the best of the week, and this is someone that we had completely overlooked in the lineup. Now Saymyname is another artist on our list that we prioritize seeing at music festivals.

If you're at a giant festival with multiple stages, go exploring! One night at EDC, we were feeling particularly restless and adventurous. There were so many amazing artists playing that night, so we decided to just totally ditch our scheduled plans to roam around the festival and only stop for fifteen to twenty minutes wherever we liked the music regardless of who the DJ was. It was a super fun night because we never felt stressed about getting to a particular place at a specific time or obligated to stay all the way through a set just because we liked the artist.

Tip 57: Minimize Phone Usage

Get off your phone! Like I've said before, some of the best times I've ever had at festivals were when I didn't have access to my cell phone. While I do like to take one or two pictures and videos a day, I have my phone away ninety-five percent of the time. There is nothing more frustrating to me than seeing people holding up their phones to record for the entire duration of a set. Like, are you even having fun standing there not dancing so as not to disturb your video? Are you really ever going to look back and watch this whole set enough times to make up for your lack of fun-having during this set? Doubt it. Enjoying the music is so much more about just being fully present at the moment. If you can't let go and dance around like a crazy person because you're too concerned about posting your perfect videos, you've wasted your money. That being said, yes, I like to record a video or two at a set if I really love the artist, and I want to capture my friends and me in that really happy moment in time. When I record, though, it's essentially a haphazard and nonsensical video of me and all of my friends dancing and bouncing around having the time of our lives. These ridiculous videos mean so much more to me because they're real memories of the amount of fun that we were having at that moment. Seriously, though, please enjoy the festival through your eyes and not your phone screen.

Tip 58: Get to the Rail for Your Favorite Artist

Lately, I've been more of a proponent of just chilling in the middle of the crowd somewhere around a group of people with great energy. I get it, though, when your favorite artist is playing, and you just want to be at the rail for that. The easiest way to get there is to go through the crowd on the sides where people are much more spread out. Slowly work your way up and into the middle. While you're doing this, do not forget your "excuse me, sorry" and "sorry, thank you." Do not ever try cutting through the middle. You will be irritated, and so will all the people who are already packed in there, like sardines that you just tried to cut in front of. If you're meeting too much resistance while trying to cut through, just stop. Getting to the front is not worth getting upset, annoying the people around you, or missing out on the fun on your way there. Often, once you get up there, everyone is just overly pushy and exasperating anyways.

Tip 59: Your Vibe Attracts your Tribe

The actual key to enjoying your time at a set is to be surrounded by incredible people that are dancing, giving you space to dance, have smiles on their faces, and are putting out good vibes. FriendShip is probably my favorite festival to date because I didn't run into a single person on that boat that wasn't kind, respectful, and cool in every way. The clientele that this event attracts is so top-notch it's genuinely unlike any festival I've ever been to. We already knew a lot of people on Ship that year from years of Holy Ship sailings, but our everyday crew was assembled from a few people we knew from previous sailings and a few people we'd just met at random sets on the first day. Even though we all lived in different cabins scattered throughout the ship, we were all so like-minded that, without ever planning to, we all ended up meeting up in the same place at the same stage every morning. To me, this is so much more fun than getting pushed around by a bunch of (sometimes totally obnoxious) people right in the front. Just have fun with your friends, and you'll start to notice that good energy and good people will begin to surround you.

___Tip 60: Let your Freak Flag Fly___

This is no world for self-consciousness and trying to be "normal." Conventional people's rules don't apply here. Stop worrying if anyone else is watching you or judging you for whatever you feel like wearing or doing. They're not. It is a world in which the more eccentric and more unique you are, the more you will shine, thrive, and feel like you belong. It may be a concept that is hard to accept for people that have never been to a festival, but it will become more effortless and more instinctual to adapt to once you're there. You'll start to notice that you get more and more immersed every day in all of the wonderful weirdness going on around you, and you'll begin to lose touch with reality more and more every day. It is awesome.

Holy Ship used to do two sailings every year; doing both sailings was referred to as "back to backing," and the whole ordeal would be seven full days of nonstop partying. Of course, I always went back to back. The last few days were always my favorite part of the festival every year because by then, I was so immersed in the world of Holy Ship that I just could not be bothered to be brought back to reality. One year, by day seven, I had somehow managed to acquire someone's giant inflatable penguin and named her Linda. I then proceeded to gallivant around Ship in my big blue fluffy OG Shipper robe, going up to everyone and making them hug Linda. You would be surprised how many people had also lost touch with reality by day seven and loved

Linda, the inflatable, hugging party penguin. I know it sounds absurd, but you just get more and more comfortable with the anything-goes mentality the longer you spend at a festival. Eventually, pretty much everybody hits their breaking point at which they are no longer even remotely concerned with the way other people perceive them. It is at this point that people become entirely free and happy. The faster you can allow yourself to get there, the more fun you will have.

Chapter 5 Summary

Live life to the fullest! Make the decision to be optimistic in every situation and to be happy every second of every day. Spread that positivity to everyone you come into contact with. Roll with the punches and never cry over spilled milk. Be spontaneous and reckless, embrace the now, and say yes. Get off your phone! Live in the moment. Allow the craziest, wildest, most carefree version of yourself to come alive, and the people you want to be a part of your tribe will come to you naturally.

Chapter 6: Act Right

Tip 61: Act with Peace

  The EDM community has a set of principles, referred to as PLUR, which everyone should be actively promoting by their actions throughout the festival. The first letter of the acronym refers to peace. Acting with peace entails avoiding conflict and negativity at all costs. It is necessary for everyone to do their part to behave peacefully at festivals to create a safe space for everyone. It is supposed to be a special, magical place that offers freedom from disturbance. At their core, Festivals are supposed to be a place where everyone puts aside their differences to coexist in an environment of friendship and consideration of others. If you're the type of person that gets easily irritated or likes to start fights, festivals are not for you. Even if you encounter one of these aggressive types at a festival, the best thing you can do is to continue to act with peace to deescalate the situation and move along. These kinds of people are not worth your time, and they are definitely not worth compromising your ease.

Tip 62: Act with Love

  The second letter in the PLUR acronym stands for love. Acting with love entails spreading warmth and positivity to everyone that you meet and doing everything you do with good intentions at heart. We all must consciously perpetuate the feeling of love so that every festival goer feels important, safe, and happy. One of the greatest joys of festivals is feeling the wholesome aura of compassion and goodwill among thousands of humans who, at that moment in time, all feel like your best friends. As with any other attitude, love has a domino effect on large groups like this. If you make one person feel loved, they'll inadvertently feel more inclined to spread that good feeling to someone else and so on until everyone at the festival is positively impacted by it.

Tip 63: Act with Unity

The third letter in the PLUR acronym refers to unity. One of the main foundations of music festivals is that we are all deeply connected to each other. It is a rare and precious realm on earth in which no matter where you are from, what religion you follow, what your ethnicity is, what your sexual preferences are, or what kind of eccentricities you have, you are at home and in a safe space. Tomorrowland is an extraordinary festival because people from over two hundred countries attend this event every year, making it the most international event on earth. When you first enter the festival, you walk underneath a giant arch with the words "Welcome Home" on it. "Home" is the perfect word to describe how you feel when you walk through that arch and into the festival. There may be hundreds of thousands of people there from all over the world, but we all feel like family, and the festival grounds feel like the home we all share.

Similarly, EDC has the slogan "All Are Welcome Here," which is displayed throughout the festival. "All are Welcome Here" is such a vibe at EDC because you really do feel like no matter how outlandish or unconventional you are, you are welcome, you are loved, you are accepted, and you are home. This unique feeling of unification is something that everyone must play an active role in maintaining by treating everyone with acceptance and love as if they are members of your own family.

Tip 64: Act with Respect

The final letter of the acronym refers to respect. First, respect the festival grounds and treat them like you would your own home. Don't throw your rubbish on the ground, do your part to keep the restrooms from getting nasty, and recycle everything you can. On Holy Ship, after every announcement, we would all shout in unison with the announcer, "Respect the Ship." This constant reminder kept us all conscious and accountable to do whatever we could not to trash or damage the ship. We all knew how lucky we were that we even had the opportunity to participate in a festival on a multi-billion dollar cruise line. Because of this, we all did our part to not tarnish our reputation as a group by disrespecting the ship to make sure that we kept this memorable experience we had going. It is an attitude that I hope to see more people practicing at future festivals—having a mindset of being conscious of and having respect for the party grounds and the people who will have to clean up after you is so important. You would be surprised at the number of people that don't seem to realize that there are trash cans at music festivals. Don't be like those people.

    Second, respect the workers at the festival. Show respect to the security guards, the bartenders, the food stand workers, the medics, etc. I'm telling you, these people are saints. The festival workers put up with more insane degenerate behavior from festival-goers than we could possibly imagine, so, whenever possible, show them a little extra love and respect. Lastly, of course, respect each other. The more respect that you give, the more you will receive in return. The utopia of the festival world relies heavily on the underlying principles of mutual respect and everyone treating each other the way they would like to be treated.

Tip 65: Share

    True festival-goers are intrinsically sharers. We share everything with each other because sharing is caring, right? Like I've said before, I like to bring extra glitter and adhesive with me to every show I go to. One year on Ship, I posted a photo on our Facebook group of all the recovery remedies and supplements I had on me and my cabin number in case someone got hungover or seasick. The response was overwhelming, and it made me feel so good to offer help to people who were hurting. At Lost Lands, I brought a bunch of extra pain patches with me for everyone suffering from extreme headbanging neck soreness. Even little things like sharing water with someone who looks thirsty or sharing your fan with someone that's overheated can make a massive difference to that person. Whatever it is that you want to share, sharing your resources with your new festival friends is one of the most rewarding parts of going to a festival.

Tip 66: Use Your Manners

When you walk through a crowd and bump into people, don't forget to say, "Please, I'm sorry, excuse me, thank you," on repeat. These little decency statements can go a long way in keeping the peace because they show the person that you've accidentally bumped into that you acknowledge them, that you respect them and that you didn't mean to bump into them. Also, please do not participate in those extremely impertinent human "trains" that put their arms on each other's shoulders, fifteen people deep, and bully their way through a crowd. It's seriously so rude, and people need to stop doing this.

Tip 67: Understand your Impact

By understanding your impact, you know the effect that your actions and words have, not only on yourself and your crew but on everyone around you as well. Be the good energy you want to see at the festival. Vibes, good or bad, have a snowball effect. If you wake up with an openly bad attitude, that is likely to at least slightly negatively affect your roommate. If both you and your roommate are in bad moods, that will likely negatively impact a lot of other people you come into contact with. Your attitude is like body glitter, in that you only meant to get it on you, but you probably spread tiny specks of it to thousands of other people that you brushed up against by the end of the night. Can you imagine a day in which every person on earth woke up and decided that they would be happy and only put out good energy that day? The world would be a beautiful and perfect place. Festivals are the closest we will ever get to that kind of an ideal world, so everyone must do their part to make sure that they shut out every thought or attitude that could adversely affect the greater good of the festival community. You are in complete control of your feelings and the vibes that you put out, so even if you're having a bad day, fake happiness until you find joy.

Chapter 6 Summary

Behave peacefully. The festival world is supposed to be a place that is free from conflict, disturbance, and negativity. Everyone must do their part to coexist peacefully and make this a safe space for everyone. Behave with love and goodwill towards all of your fellow festival-goers. Think about your actions and do everything you do with good intentions at heart. Behave in a manner of unity with everyone around you. We are all deeply connected in the festival world. It is a special space in which it does not matter where you are from, what religion you follow, what your sexual preferences are, what your political views are, and so on because you are home here. We must put all of our differences aside in the festival world to love and accept everyone we encounter. Finally, behave with respect. Respect the festival grounds, respect the festival workers, and respect each other. Everyone must play an active role in perpetuating all of these mannerisms to keep the festival world as pure and idealistic as possible.

Chapter 7: Settling in and Making Friends

Tip 68: Organize Your Belongings in Your Accommodation Immediately

I am admittedly notorious for just flinging my belongings all over my accommodation in a fierce angst to get dressed up to run out to play. Because of this, I spend the rest of my mornings trying to find where the different parts of my outfits and accessories are, only to frequently end up improvising and throwing together whatever I see on the floor first. This is bad, don't do this. It will be the calmest, cleanest, and most organized your life will be for a few days, so use it to your advantage. Even just taking ten minutes to lay all of your outfits and accessories out together day by day will help you tremendously once you enter into party mode for the next few days.

Tip 69: Mark your Tent

If you are camping, you will be significantly less dazed and confused when you reach the campsite of thousands of matching tents if you mark your tent. Suppose my neighbors at Tomorrowland hadn't put up a helium-infused unicorn above their tent. In that case, I have absolutely no idea how I would've found it the night I got separated from the group without a phone (which contained my tent number). I am forever indebted to that unicorn. People do all kinds of cool things to their tents, though, like country flags, string lights, mandala pareos, the list goes on. I've also found it very helpful to write my room or tent number on the inside of my arm in Sharpie, along with my roommate's phone number.

__Tip 70: Lock your Tent__

I know I've spent a lot of time talking about how pure and kind the festival community is, but you have to keep in mind that there is bound to be at least one rogue miscreant in gatherings of this size that is only there to take advantage of trusting humans. These kinds of deplorable people are few and far between, so be cautious, but not worried. While tents are easily slashed through, enough people leave their tents unlocked that these kinds of unsavory people will usually go for the more easily accessible tents. To this day, I have still never had anyone break into my tent because I always keep it locked.

__Tip 71: Make Friends with your Neighbors__

Your neighbors may become some of your closest friends at the festival, so introduce yourself and become best friends as soon as possible! Holy Ship and FriendShip are two of the coolest festivals to meet your neighbors at because you share balconies overlooking the ocean. It's so much fun because at all times, you have rooms above you, below you, and to the sides of you that are out having their early morning after parties or afternoon breakfast champagne to start the day, so you're never alone when you step out there. My neighbors from my Ship sailings have become some of my best friends in my life to this day. At Tomorrowland, we had the perfect neighbor tent circle ever. The American girls brought our glitter to share, the Swiss boys brought their giant speaker for constant party tunes, and the Irish boys brought their jokes and relentlessly good vibes. It was one of the best experiences I've had with neighbors at a festival in my life. Your neighbors are the only people at the whole festival that you are guaranteed to see every single day, so take advantage of that relationship and make best friends forever with your neighbors right away!

__Tip 72: Talk to Everyone__

Seriously, do not be afraid to talk to people! Get out of your comfort zone and put yourself out there. If you want to make new friends, this is the perfect place. Festival people are the easiest people to talk to in the world. Just the fact that you're at the same festivals means that you probably already have a lot in common. I've made so many friends at festivals in random places like standing in line for a drink or getting ready in the bathrooms. It can be as simple as telling someone that you like their outfit to spark up a conversation or asking them what their favorite set so far has been or who they're most excited to see. I don't think I've ever started a conversation with someone at a festival that didn't want to chat it up as well. You just never know when that random stranger you talked to could end up being totally awesome and one of your new favorite festival friends. So take advantage of the fact that you're in this party paradise with thousands of magnificent like-minded people and make as many connections as you can. The party will end at some point, but the friendships you keep never will.

Tip 73: Trade Contact info

You will meet so many people every day at festivals, and at the larger ones, you may never run into those people again for the rest of that festival. If you meet someone you like, don't forget to grab their social media so you can keep up with them after the festival is over. You may not have reception wherever you are, so it's easier to start a note on your phone and type down people's information in there and search for them after the festival. Post-festival-you will thank festival-you for keeping up with these people to share photos, videos, memories, etc. Making these kinds of connections will be very beneficial if you're a traveler too. On my last trip to Europe, I had friends in every city that I visited because I chose to keep up with the people I met. Who knows, I could still be standing in that massive line outside of "De School" in Amsterdam (or worse, I might have never known it even existed) and missed out on one of my favorite nights of my life had I not made it a point to keep up with my friend that I met in the Philippines.

Tip 74: Get your Fanny Pack or Hydration Backpack Ready

Before you enter the festival, do one final fanny pack or backpack check. My fanny pack always contains my ID, sunglasses, SPF Chapstick (unopened), SPF powder, a Liquid IV hydration packet, protective earplugs, cell phone, glitter with adhesive, a little cash, a credit card in a secret pocket, a travel-sized pack of sealed antibacterial wipes, and a few Band-Aids. Along with my fanny pack, I also always have a rain jacket and a hand fan. My boyfriend always carries the three-liter hydration backpack for us. Whatever you think you'll need, make a checklist and always go through it before you leave for the festival because once you're in there, it's going to be a giant, time-consuming pain to head back to your accommodation to retrieve said forgotten item later.

If you find that your list of items you want to bring to the festival is way more than you want to carry around with you all day, many festivals have lockers that you can rent for the day. These lockers are fantastic for storing things like heavy water bottles, bulky sweaters, and other warm clothing for when it gets cold at night and all of your awesome new festival merch that you don't want to carry around with you all night.

___Tip 75: Familiarize yourself with the Festival Grounds___

I like to get through the festival gates as early as possible to explore around with the map so that I know where everything is before it gets dark and hectic in there. The most important places to locate are the restrooms, the free water refill station, the medical tent, bars, and food stands. The very first thing you should do is go straight to the free water station and fill up your hydration pack so that you don't have to worry about that for several hours. If you ask nicely, many vendors will also give you free ice to keep your water cold. It'll be way easier to gain your bearings right away when the festival isn't at capacity, and you're the most clear-minded. You don't want to put yourself in the position of desperately looking for the water station at 2 am when you're already a little dazed by the party. The water lines can get very long, though, so definitely don't wait until you're super thirsty to get water. Besides showing up early to situate yourself, another good reason to show up early is to get through security more seamlessly. The people working security put up with a lot throughout the day, and I can promise you that they will be more lenient and way less agitated at the beginning of the day than after a few hours on the job.

___Tip 76: Set an Emergency Meeting Spot___

No matter how careful you are all being about keeping to the buddy system and not separating, it's not unheard of for someone to take off and accidentally get lost (I would know because this person is usually me). This person may not mean to run, be we get excitable sometimes! So, in case you have a runner on your hands and cannot get cell reception, set up a meeting spot somewhere in the festival that you all agree to go back to if someone is missing for more than twenty minutes (or however long you all decide is too long). My best advice would be to choose some sort of infrastructure that's super tall with bright lights that's a little more on the outskirts rather than smack dab in the middle of the festival. If you set a meeting spot right in the center of the party, it will still be difficult for everyone to find each other even though you're all in the same area. Another tip to try to stay connected with your friends a little better is to timestamp all of your text messages. For example, typing, "In the back left at Dillon Francis 1:20 am". Generally, it is tough to get reception at festivals, and you won't receive a message from your friend for several hours after it has been sent, so timestamp to avoid confusion.

Tip 77: Get Up Early to Get Ready or Go to the Salons

If you're camping and want to take the time to do intricate hair or makeup, I highly recommend getting to the bathrooms as early as possible. Festival bathrooms get really nasty very quickly, so if you want a clean space to get ready in, don't sleep in. If you can handle it for a few days, though, it's honestly just easier to take a baby wipe shower and get ready outside of your tent. If you adamantly want your hair to be washed and styled every day and don't have the energy to do it yourself, there will be salons available at a lot of camps and inside most festivals. The salons are a little pricey, but if you have the extra money, they're a total lifesaver when you don't feel like brushing through your dreading party hair, but you still want to look fresh and pretty. I finally took advantage of this for the first time on my last day of FriendShip. I woke feeling like I had been hit by a bus, my hair was almost completely dreaded, and my shaky hands were no match for my untamed mane. I threw in the towel (or hairbrush, in this case) and made an appointment at the beauty bar downstairs, at which a lovely man named Raul from India spent over an hour detangling, washing, and styling my hair. It was honestly the best seventy-five dollars I think I've ever spent at a festival.

Chapter 7 Summary

Organize your tent, mark your tent, and lock your tent. Get up early to make good use of the restrooms while they're still clean. Get to the festival early to locate free water stations, bathrooms, the medical tent, bars, and food stands. Most importantly, make connections! There are thousands of incredible, unique people to meet at music festivals. Take advantage of the fact that you are in this party haven with all these extraordinary individuals and make as many friends as possible. Festival people are so easy to talk to because we all just want to meet new people and chat it up too! It's as simple as telling someone that you're standing next to in line for drinks that you love their outfit or asking people that you're in line with to get into the festival which artists they're most excited to see. It doesn't even matter what you say; just strike up conversations and make friends wherever you go because the festival will end at some point, but you will hold onto the friends you make there forever.

Chapter 8: Keeping yourself and your Friends Safe

Tip 78: Know your Limits

Do everything in moderation. Not that I condone any type of overindulgence anywhere in general, but music festivals are quite possibly the worst place to overindulge. For example, if you're not much of a drinker, don't pick now to start taking shots with people. For one, you'll probably either get sick or blackout, and both of those options are super lame for you. For another, now you've ruined at least one of your friend's nights because someone has to take care of you now, and that's just rude. These are far from the worst-case scenarios you could land yourself in by overindulging, so be cool to yourself and your friends and don't overdo any of it.

Tip 79: Know When to Take a Breather

If you find yourself starting to feel light-headed or sick, listen to your body and take a friend with you out of the crowd for a breather. Sit down in the grass, drink some water, and rest until you feel good again. Don't push yourself until you pass out. Your friends will be way more into chilling in the grass with you for a little bit than having to come to find you in the medic tent later. Don't forget that this is a marathon, and you will have to take a few water breaks to make it to the finish line.

__Tip 80: Stick to your Buddy System__

Buddy systems are for better or for worse. Even if your favorite artist is playing your favorite song, if your buddy feels like they need to step out and sit down, you or someone else in your crew should go with them. Yes, sometimes you'll be vibing and not be ready to go, but you would want them to go with you. It can be super tempting just to let your friend go off alone, but as I've said before, it is surprisingly easy to lose people even if you have eyes on where they were going the whole time. It's easier to just stick with your friends than being lost and alone trying to find your friends later. Never feel bad about asking someone to go with you; your friends will care more about your well-being than be annoyed with you needing to take a break. In turn, always be prepared to take care of your friends and be willing to go sit down with them when they're hurting too. Never let someone feel alone or guilty because they need to chill for a second. We're all human, and your friends are far more important than whatever set you're at.

__Tip 81: Keep your Belongings Safe__

I cannot stress this enough, If you're bringing a fanny pack in, always make sure it is turned around so that you can see it the whole time. Don't put valuables in your pockets either; this is a very easy place for things to fall out of or other people to take something out of. Try to stash your valuable objects (money, phones, Go-Pros, etc.) into the deepest, darkest, least accessible part of your fanny pack or hydration backpack. One up-and-coming company that I recommend looking into is The Lunch Box Backpacks. This brand makes insulated, light-up, two-liter bladder hydration packs designed specifically to make it extremely difficult for thieves to take anything out of them. Thefts are pretty few and far between, but they do happen, so it's better just to be safe and aware than sorry and phone-less, wallet-less, and so on.

Tip 82: Don't Take Drinks from Strangers

Again, people with bad intentions aren't super common at festivals, but they are still there. If you meet a stranger and they want to buy you a drink, awesome! Go to the bar with them and grab your drink straight from the bartender. If said stranger has only good intentions, then they won't have an issue with that. If a stranger randomly just comes up to you and hands you a drink, and you don't want to be rude (just in case it actually isn't brimming with roofies), just hold onto it until you find a place where you can discreetly dump it. Better to be drink-less than roofied.

Tip 83: Don't Take Drugs from Strangers

I shouldn't have to say this, but just don't do it. Seriously, this is how people die at festivals. You have no idea what the dosage is or what kind of rogue unexpected mystery substance could be in there. You also don't know what kind of reaction it could have with what's already in your system. Recently, there has been a pretty scary crisis of the prescription painkiller fentanyl, making it into a lot of designer festival drugs, especially cocaine. This drug, created initially to be a pain killer, can be lethal at certain dosages. Drug dealers are cutting their products with it to maximize their profits, and kids all over the world have started dying of fentanyl overdoses at parties. The fentanyl crisis is one of the many examples I could give you for how bad of an idea it is to take these kinds of chances on mystery drugs at festivals. Taking drugs from strangers is like gambling with your life; there is a chance it could be fun, but you could end up in the hospital or dead, just as easily.

Disclaimer: In no way do I condone or encourage drug use at festivals. That being said, in the interest of being transparent and realistic, drug use is not uncommon at music festivals. If you do choose to do drugs, please do so safely and in moderation. Ravesafe.org is an excellent resource for anyone who wants more information on this subject. The people working on this website state that they do not condone or condemn drug use; they just want everyone to be as informed and educated as possible.

Tip 84: Remember to Eat

It can be a struggle to stop and remember to eat when there is always something more fun going on somewhere else, and you're too distracted even to realize that you're hungry. At some point, though, forgetting to eat will catch up to you. As I mentioned before, the easiest way to get quick energy right away in the mornings is through a protein bar, bag of nuts, or any food with a lot of carbs and protein. While you're at the festival, though, you need to eat at least one more time throughout the day so that you have the energy to keep on dancing all night and into the morning. Carbohydrates will be your best friend here. Carbs are a quick fuel to your muscles that give you the power to keep going until the end of the last set. Festivals are one of the few special times in your life in which you can live off of pizza, grilled cheese, giant pretzels, and so on all day, and your body will actually use all of those carbs up for energy instead of converting them to fat, so live it up! It's also super important to try to get some protein throughout the day, especially if you're drinking alcohol, because it slows the absorption of alcohol into your system.

Tip 85: Learn to Love the Smoothie Stand

Smoothies are probably my favorite food at any music festival. During summer festivals, you will almost always wake up feeling hot, so that cold smoothie is such a refreshing treat right away in the mornings. I'm also not much of a breakfast eater, to begin with, and am usually at least slightly queasy in the mornings at festivals, so I turn to smoothies because they're an excellent source of healthy and easy to consume energy. All of the vitamins and antioxidants in smoothies are a great way to add a little boost to your immune system before you head out to the party for the day as well. Most smoothie stands will also offer helpful supplements to add to your smoothies, such as energy boost, immune system boost, or protein boost. Try to go for smoothies that are all real fruit because the others contain the nutritional equivalent of drinking a cup of sugar and sorbet, which is not helpful at all.

Tip 86: Keep Hydrating

Dehydration is quite possibly the most significant health risk at any music festival, so I'm going to keep saying this because hydration is the key to wellness here. Again, I would always suggest drinking a hydration boost, such as Liquid IV, right away in the morning before your first breakfast drink and at night before you go to bed. I even like to have a packet in my fanny pack in case I start feeling super dehydrated while I'm at the festival. If you are sweating a lot and feeling thirsty, electrolyte heavy drinks like Gatorade or Powerade can be helpful as well. Another product that I swear by is Pedialyte. I've woken up thinking there was no way I could possibly continue to go on, and by the time I get to the bottom of the Pedialyte bottle, I, in effect, feel wonderful. If you can remember to drink a whole bottle before you go to sleep at night, I can almost assure you that you're going to have a pleasant morning the next day. Pedialyte is less widely available but much more highly effective than other electrolyte replenishing drinks because it has a balance of sodium and sugar to replenish the body more efficiently. Pedialyte also contains zinc, one of the best mineral supplements to enforce immune system strength.

Another surprising way to get some extra hydration is to chase your shots with pickle juice if you're drinking alcohol. Pickle juice is intensely hydrating, it prevents and treats muscle cramps, and it's loaded with antioxidants. Pickle juice tastes delicious as a chaser for whiskey shots, so if you're going to be pregaming before heading into the festival, Jameson (my favorite whiskey with pickle juice) with a pickleback is one of your healthiest options. Another way to get some extra hydration in along with the alcohol you're already drinking is to look for cocktails with coconut water in them. Coconut water is loaded with potassium, an incredibly beneficial electrolyte necessary for your muscles to contract. You can also get some extra potassium by choosing a smoothie with real bananas in it.

Aside from all of this, the easiest and cheapest way to stay hydrated is to bring in a hydration backpack into the festival, locate the free water fill station and just keep sipping all night long. Always remember that being thirsty is a sign that you're already dehydrated, so don't wait until you're thirsty because by then, it's already too late.

Tip 87: Sleep Whenever Possible

It's going to be tempting to try to find ways not just to sleep the whole time, but even if you can only squeeze in a few hours at a time, it will help you immensely. There will rarely be a time when there is absolutely nothing you want to do, so prioritizing is necessary. Just be careful to set alarms before the next big thing you're excited to go to because you're probably going to be exhausted, and you might just accidentally keep sleeping through it. Sleep is essential, though, to keep your energy levels up and your immune system going strong.

Chapter 8 Summary

Your safety and the safety of the people around you is the most important thing to be concerned about at any given moment during the festival. The most important thing that you can do to stay safe is to stay hydrated. Bring a hydration backpack into the festival, take sips from it all night long, use hydration multiplying powders to make your water work harder, drink Pedialyte, chase your shots with pickle juice, and drink cocktails with coconut water. Aside from making sure to hydrate, also remember to keep your belongings tucked away and close to your body. Be smart, and don't take drugs or drinks from strangers. Remember that you have to eat and rest to be a fully functioning human. Most importantly, take care of your friends and have their backs because if everyone looks out for each other, you will all have a better experience at the festival.

Part 3: After the Party

Unfortunately, the party always has to end eventually, and we all have to return to our regular lives. By the end of most festivals, you will probably find yourself feeling at least a little sick, tired, and just downright sad that it's all over. This segment of the festival is never fun for anybody. Still, after many years and many festivals, I've come up with a list of actions that make surviving the festival come down much less physically and emotionally painful. In this part, I will go over the many different coping mechanisms that I use to help heal my mind and body quickly and efficiently so that I can start planning for my next festival adventure as soon as possible.

Chapter 9: Heal your Body

Tip 88: Replenish your Body with Healthy Foods

When you get home, eat foods that work with your body, not against it. You'll probably find yourself scarfing down a buttery mac and cheese stuffed grilled cheese sandwich at 4 am more than once at the festival. That's festival life, and that's okay because your body needs that energy-dense carbohydrate rush to keep going. Chances are you're probably not sitting down for a nutrient-rich veggie-filled salad even once during the festival. Again, it is all fine for a short time because you're working out twelve to twenty hours a day. Once you get home, though, your body will be begging you for some seriously replenishing nutrition. I like to reach for foods that detox and cleanse my body from all of the bacteria I've been exposed to and junk food I've consumed. Some of the best detox foods include broccoli, asparagus, artichoke, ginger, turmeric, nuts and seeds, berries, lemon, garlic, and beets. One quick and delicious way to get all of those veggies and garlic into one meal is to make a stir fry. Homemade smoothies with lots of fresh fruit and lemon juice pack a great detoxifying punch as well. Some other superfoods to consider adding extra to your diet include fish, leafy greens, whole grains, tomatoes, olive oil, and legumes.

Tip 89: Continue to Hydrate

For the last time, the best way to get your body back up to 100% and help clear out all of those unneeded toxins in your system is to flush it out with water. I get it; water isn't super fun; it's just not. I have a tough time drinking plain water, so I have a few tricks in my arsenal to get myself to enjoy drinking it. MiO drops are a simple way to make water taste like anything but water so that you'll want to drink more of it. These drops come in various delicious flavors and are available in four different versions: Original, Energy, Electrolyte, and Vitamin. Another great way to get some extra delicious hydration after the party is through decaffeinated detox teas. My favorite brand of detox tea is Yogi Tea. They have several different flavors that all taste so good and have such superb cleansing effects on your body.

Tip 90: Catch up on Sleep

Catching up on sleep is one of the biggest reasons that I suggest taking a few days off after the festival whenever possible. You will probably find yourself incredibly drained once the excitement wears down and you're on your way back home. When I get home from festivals, I almost always end up sleeping for ten to twelve hours at a time my first couple of nights home. Your body and mind are in serious recovery mode at this point. When your body tells you it needs something, it's usually best to listen to it. You'll be amazed at how restored you feel in the morning after twelve hours of uninterrupted sleep after a festival. Nothing feels better than turning your phone off, drawing the blackout curtains, cranking the AC, and drifting off, knowing you have nowhere to be the next day. I like to have a couple of days of this blissful nothingness and alone time, but even if you can only afford to give yourself one day, do it by any means possible.

__Tip 91: Go Back to the Chiropractor__

If you've done your research since Part One and have decided that a chiropractor visit is something that would benefit you, try to have an appointment already set up for when you get back. You'll be forcing your body into a lot of abnormal movements for extended periods while you're out being wild at the party, so a quick readjustment will feel really good when you get home.

__Tip 92: Go Back to Yoga__

Yoga is a fantastic way to center your mind and body before a festival, but its positive effects are just as rewarding during the recovery period. Festivals take a considerable toll on your body. The chances are that no matter what you've done to prepare physically, you'll probably come home at least a little sore and hurting—cue yoga. Using yoga to soothe and stretch out sore muscles is as easy as typing "yoga for sore muscles" into a search engine. Although it is grueling, now is also a perfect time to try out hot yoga to purge all of those festival toxins out of your body. If you're experiencing post-festival sadness at all, yoga can also help with that in that it is a proven way to ease your mind, reduce stress, and improve feelings of well-being and self-efficacy.

<u>Tip 93: Get a Thai Massage</u>

Okay, full disclosure, this will probably be the least relaxing massage of your life, but it will work wonders on an achy body. Thai massage is a traditional healing practice that uses pressure and stretching techniques to rejuvenate and restore your body. I genuinely consider these massage therapists to be healers because they individually tune the massage they give you to what they feel is off in your body. Like a typical massage, they work on every body part one by one, but they feel each body part first for problem areas. Once they start working on that part of the body, it can be pretty painful because if they feel anything off, they will pay special attention to that area until it feels synchronized with the rest of your body again. While there are relaxing moments, for the most part, these massages are supposed to be at least a little bit painful. However, the glorious moment comes when you walk out of the massage feeling like a completely brand new human. There is no soreness that a Thai massage has yet to deliver me from. If you're feeling hopelessly in pain after the party, brace yourself, book a Thai massage, and expect to feel fantastic once it's all over.

Chapter 9 Summary

When you get home from a festival, your body is likely to be pretty depleted of nutrients and energy. The most important thing you can do to restore your body quickly is to catch up on sleep immediately. Along with getting enough sleep, you will need to nourish your body with detoxifying and cleansing foods and supplements such as fruits, veggies, detox teas, echinacea, zinc, garlic, and turmeric. If your muscles are sore or you're just feeling physically unbalanced in general, going to the chiropractor, doing yoga, and getting a Thai massage are all excellent ways to help you to heal your body as well.

Chapter 10: Heal Your Mind

Tip 94: Take a Reset Vacation from your Vacation

You've just come from a sparkling world of surreal freedom and bliss. By the last day, you've probably become so enmeshed with the lively, outlandish, and imaginative culture of the festival world that you're finding the real world somewhat challenging to readjust to. Returning to normality after these breathtaking moments in your life is never an easy transition. Sometimes, I return home from festivals feeling hopelessly depressed. I start to resent real life for all of the ways that it differs from festival life. People around me bore me, my job bores me, and I am in disbelief that it's still not socially acceptable for me to coat myself in glitter every single day. It is why I recommend taking a small vacation after your festival trip. Give yourself at least one day to sleep, decompress, and accept the fact that you have to go back to work and readjust to everyday life.

If you're lucky enough to get more than one extra day off to readjust, one thing I would highly recommend doing is unpacking, doing laundry, and cleaning up your living space in general. Having an immaculate living space is so good for your mental health that it reduces stress and makes you feel more clear-minded and relaxed in your home. Take it from someone who has been known to refuse to unpack from a trip for up to weeks at a time: it's realistically not going to take you that long, and you're going to feel immeasurably calmer and more at peace in your space once it is clean. After you're done cleaning, light a candle, read a good book, watch a movie that you love, or do whatever it is that you enjoy doing to unwind, and just savor the quiet time to yourself.

Tip 95: Meditate

Again, it can be challenging to keep a positive mindset after you've returned from a blissful week of nonstop good times. I often leave festivals feeling like there is no possible way I could ever have that much fun again. I can never realize it at the time, but this thought is totally ridiculous and untrue. Daily meditation can help you focus on the present, decrease negative thoughts and feelings, lower stress, promote a more realistic perspective on life, and guide the mind toward creativity. While the benefits of meditation vary from person to person, meditating helps me out of negative or stressful mindsets in that I always come out feeling more grounded, clear-minded, and optimistic. If you've never tried it before, meditating can truthfully be quite tricky, so don't give up if you can't conquer it right away. My best advice for beginners just learning to meditate is to be alone, turn off any stimulants (TV, phone, etc.) around you, sit or lay down in a comfortable position and focus on the movements of your breathing as you inhale and exhale slowly. Your mind is likely to wander, so just be patient with yourself and bring yourself back to your breathing pattern when you notice this beginning to happen. Don't give up when your mind strays; this is part of the practice. When you want to come out of your meditative state, do so slowly and consciously, paying attention to the present moment and how you currently feel. The practice of meditation is such a helpful tool to get you out of a bad headspace and into moments of real clarity and peace.

Tip 96: Spend Time Outside

Another way to beat the post-festival blues and jet lag is to go outside and get as much sunshine as possible. After many days of sleeping for two to four hours at a time, sometimes in the middle of the day and sometimes in the middle of the morning, and sometimes in a foreign time zone, your body will be tremendously confused. Solving internal clock confusion can be as simple as just forcing yourself to be outside during the day. If you did take a little bit of time off to readjust, the simple act of doing whatever you were going to do inside (read, watch Netflix, whatever) outside instead will slowly start to help you reacclimate.

Another benefit of spending time outdoors is that fresh air and sunshine are good for the mind and soul. Getting fresh air is good for you for so many reasons, including improving mental clarity and energy levels, helping the body to heal faster, strengthening the immune system, and increasing serotonin levels. Time spent outside in the sun is perhaps the most beneficial in the festival recovery process. Moderate sunlight exposure enhances your mood, improves sleep, reduces stress, and reinforces the immune system's strength.

Tip 97: Boost your Endorphins

Endorphins are neurotransmitters in the human body that works with your opioid receptors to help you cope with pain or stress and induce feelings of euphoria. Endorphins, to put it simply, are essentially your body's natural feel-good chemical. There are many ways to boost your endorphins naturally, including exercise, laughing, meditation, yoga, receiving a massage, and even eating dark chocolate and spicy foods. Going for long hikes outside is my favorite way not only to spend time outdoors but to boost my endorphins as well. Whichever method works best for you, an endorphin boost can do wonders for your mental health after returning home from a festival.

Tip 98: Return to Normality ASAP

Taking a few days off after a festival is incredibly healing, but if you take too many days off, you're likely to get stuck in a vicious cycle of feeling sad and missing festival life. At the end of the day, getting back into your ordinary routine will help bring you back to reality and remind you that you work hard every day to afford to go to festivals whenever you want. It can be tough not to sulk after a festival; you've just had the best time of your life, feeling the love, beauty, and freedom all around you only to return to your seemingly monotonous job and life.

Keep in mind, though, that you are in complete control of how you react to this feeling.

In my experience, the best way to deal with this is to just get back into the swing of things and find little things to be grateful for in my everyday life. I like to make gratitude lists when I'm feeling down to help remind myself about all of the amazing things in my life that I need to be more appreciative of. All you have to do is write down what you're grateful for and revisit that list at least once a day or whenever you feel sad. The points on these lists can be as simple as "I have amazing friends that love me" or "I have an awesome dog." List anything that you can look at in your life as a positive. Every time I feel down, I revisit my gratitude list and feel instantly better. Suppose I start to feel sorry for myself because I have to go to work. In that case, I review that list and realize that two of my most significant points on that list are that I have an excellent job in a beautiful spot on the water in Hawai'i, and I get to work with a lot of people that I enjoy spending time with. When I put it like that, I realize that my reality is truthfully pretty awesome and something that I am immensely grateful for. No matter your situation, finding the positives in it will do wonders for your mental health.

__Tip 99: Stay in Touch with your Festival Friends__

Staying in touch with your new friends is one of the best ways to beat the festival blues because the festival may be over, but your friendships can last a lifetime if you put the work into them. The easiest way to keep in touch with the multitude of people you'll meet at festivals is through social media. In this day and age, pretty much everyone you meet will have an Instagram account, and it's much more interactive than using platforms like Facebook or Twitter. Even if you don't like to use social media a lot, it is the best way to preserve long-distance friendships with people that you may only see at festivals a few days out of the year. It's nice to be able to send an "Awesome meeting you at the festival, hope you're adjusting back to real life okay!" type of message to check in with your new friends who are probably missing festival life just as much as you are. Most people who go to festivals go to multiple festivals throughout the year, so it's not unlikely that you'll start to party with the same people again and again.

<u>Tip 100: Keep your Festival Glow Going</u>

Often, you'll come home from a festival feeling totally high on life. Alacrity and joy just ooze out your pores to the point that you almost visibly gleam with happiness from your experiences at the festival. If you can hold onto this feeling and transfer this elated, altruistic mindset into your regular life, you'll find yourself being unbothered by things that used to upset you. You'll probably find yourself positively affecting the people around you, and therefore your reality, as well. This light inside of you can be challenging to hold onto once you enter back into the real world, but it's something that you have complete control to decide to do, and it's so much more fun than holding onto post-festival sadness. As someone who struggled a lot with reintegrating into real life after a festival, I've been trying to practice this idea a lot lately. I can absolutely say that deciding to bask in the beautiful memory of the festival instead of sulking that it is over has improved my life significantly between festivals. One easy way to do this is to keep yourself involved in the music scene at home. Going to shows and meeting like-minded people in your city can help bring you to the realization that you can still have fun outside of the festival world.

Tip 101: Start Planning your Next Adventure

Planning my next holiday is always my favorite way of overcoming post-festival depression. I find that if I start planning my next trip immediately upon returning home, I will always have something to be excited about, and eager people who are planning trips have no time to be sad. Keeping my calendar packed full of fun events to look forward to keeps me sane. Always having so many events planned keeps me way more financially responsible as well. I'm smarter with my spending habits, and my work ethic skyrockets when I know I have something coming up that will be far more fun than going out to the bars with my friends every night. It is likely that after your first festival, you're going to want to live in the festival world forever, so stay focused, keep your priorities straight, and work hard to keep the party going.

Chapter 10 Summary

One of the most challenging aspects of attending a music festival is the inexplicable sadness you may feel when you come home. It's almost like a comedown from being too high on life. Some methods that I use to help improve my mental clarity and stability are taking a few days off to recenter, meditating every day, spending time outside, making a gratitude list, and boosting my endorphins. It always helps to talk to people about how you're feeling; this is a perfect time to reach out to the friends you've made at the festival who are probably missing festival life just as much as you are. Above all else, I think that getting excited about another festival trip can be the most beneficial in keeping your spirits up after a festival.

Conclusion

Woo! You made it through the guidebook! I know, It's a lot to ingest, but if you consider these tips and learn from my numerous mistakes, I know that you will have a fantastic time at your next festival. My hope for you is that after reading this guidebook, you're feeling inspired to finally book that ticket to the festival of your dreams. I hope that you are feeling more confident and more prepared to take on your next festival. I hope that you remember to hydrate, feel free to be yourself, and treat everyone around you with kindness and love. I hope that you return home safe and healthy, with a sparkle in your eye, more motivated than ever to plan your next adventure. I hope to see you all on the dance floor somewhere in the world soon!

About the Expert

Lydia Endel attended the University of Hawai'i at Manoa, at which she graduated with a BA degree in English Literature. She now lives in Honolulu, Hawai'i, and spends her time writing, traveling the world, and attending as many music festivals as possible along the way. You can keep up with her on Instagram @lydia.endel to follow her past and present travels and music festival adventures.

HowExpert publishes quick 'how to' guides on all topics from A to Z by everyday experts. Visit HowExpert.com to learn more.

Recommended Resources

- HowExpert.com – Quick 'How To' Guides on All Topics from A to Z by Everyday Experts.
- HowExpert.com/free – Free HowExpert Email Newsletter.
- HowExpert.com/books – HowExpert Books
- HowExpert.com/courses – HowExpert Courses
- HowExpert.com/clothing – HowExpert Clothing
- HowExpert.com/membership – HowExpert Membership Site
- HowExpert.com/affiliates – HowExpert Affiliate Program
- HowExpert.com/writers – Write About Your #1 Passion/Knowledge/Expertise & Become a HowExpert Author.
- HowExpert.com/resources – Additional HowExpert Recommended Resources
- YouTube.com/HowExpert – Subscribe to HowExpert YouTube.
- Instagram.com/HowExpert – Follow HowExpert on Instagram.
- Facebook.com/HowExpert – Follow HowExpert on Facebook.

Made in the USA
Columbia, SC
12 April 2023